PICTURE KNITS

PICTURE
KNITS

EASY DESIGNS FOR THE
NOVICE KNITTER

BETTY BARNDEN

kp books
An imprint of F+W Publications, Inc.
888-457-2873

kp books
An imprint of F+W Publications, Inc.
888-457-2873

A Quarto Book

First published in North America in 2005 by
KP Books
700 East State Street
Iola, WI 54990-0001

Library of Congress Catalog Card Number
2005924813
ISBN 0-89689-153-4

QUAR.EKN

Conceived, designed, and produced by
Quarto Publishing plc
The Old Brewery
6 Blundell Street
London N7 9BH

Project Editor Paula McMahon
Art Editor Tim Pattinson
Copy Editor Eleanor Holme
Designer Louise Clements
Illustrator Coral Mula
Assistant Art Director Penny Cobb
Photographers Phil Wilkins, Paul Forrester
Proofreader Tracie Davis
Indexer Pamela Ellis

Art Director Moira Clinch
Publisher Paul Carslake

Manufactured by Provision (Pte) Ltd,
Singapore
Printed by Star Standard Industries (Pte),
Singapore

9 8 7 6 5 4 3 2 1

CONTENTS

Motif index

Small heart 94

Double heart 94

Two hearts 94

Large heart 95

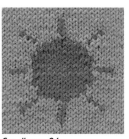
Small sun 96

Moon 96

Small star 96

Large sun 97

Large stars 98

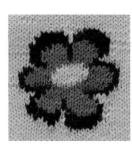
Cosmos 99

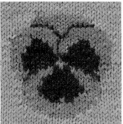
Pansy 99

Lily 99

Large roses 100

Small rose 101

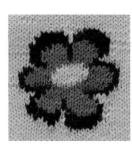
Peony 101

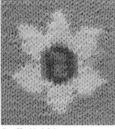
Daffodil 101

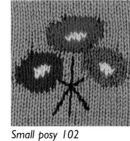
Small posy 102

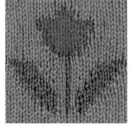
Small tulip 102

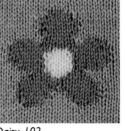
Daisy 102

Large tulips 103

Flowerpot 104

Large posy 105

Apple 106

Cherries 106

Strawberries 106

Tree 107

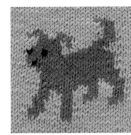
Small dog 108

Cat 108

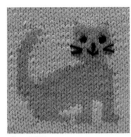
Rabbit 108

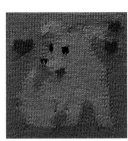
Love my dog 109

Duck 110

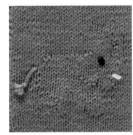
Small elephant 110

Mouse 110

Large elephant 111

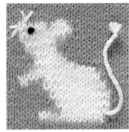
Small butterfly 112

Bird 112

Bee 112

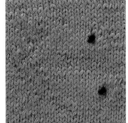
Large butterfly 113

Small fish 114

Snake 114

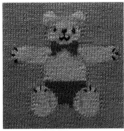
Frog 114

Large fish 115

Small ted 116

Balloons 116

Kite 116

Large ted 117

Boat 118

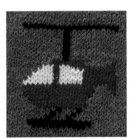

Plane 118

Helicopter 118

Pirate ship 119

Alphabet 120

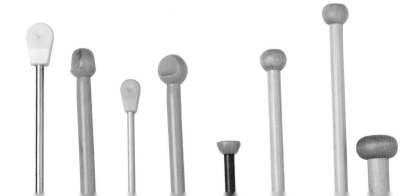

About this book

Learn how to make fun, colorful knits for your family and home, or as gifts for friends. Picture knitting (also known as "intarsia" knitting) looks complicated, but once you have learned a few basic skills you will find it really isn't that tricky at all.

Begin with a simple heart or star motif and progress to flowers, animals, and lettering. All the motifs are worked from charts, and once you understand how to read these, you can see at a glance how your work is progressing.

Begin by browsing through Knitting Know-how, to refresh your memory on the basic knitting moves. All the techniques needed to make the projects

in the book are described here, and shown in photographs, from choosing yarns and needles through casting on, basic stitches, shaping and binding off to assembling garments, working buttonholes and borders and adding trims. Follow these basic methods for a professional finish to your knitting.

In the Picture Knitting section you will find all the techniques you need to knit pictures from charts explained in detail. Starting with the simplest designs, we guide you through adding embroidered details, using textured yarns and stitches, and placing a motif on a pattern of your choice, all clearly illustrated with step-by-step photographs and diagrams. Each group of techniques is followed by one or more projects for you to knit, using the methods you have just learned. The projects are graded in order of the time and skills required, from a simple purse, scarf, or pull-on hat, through cushions and other accessories, to sweater patterns for babies, children, and teens.

You can substitute your own choice of

picture from the Motif Gallery on any of these projects. We also show you how to place a motif on any suitable knitting pattern, so you can make whatever garment you want, adding one or more motifs wherever you wish.

The Motif Gallery contains over 50 charts—hearts, flowers, animals, toys, and more; you'll find something here to suit any member of your family. All the charts are in color, and we've added a simple system of symbols to guide you along the way. The motifs are charted in one of two sizes: all the small motifs are the same size and are therefore interchangeable, and so are all the larger ones. This gives you a wide choice when knitting your projects—in any project from this book you can substitute a same-size chart for the one we used in the knitted example. You can knit these pictures in your own choice of colors and yarns onto projects from the book, or add them to other knitting patterns. We include charted lettering, so you can add a name or slogan to your knitting. We also provide a blank grid and show you how to draw your own charts, so you can knit any crazy picture you want—the only limit is your imagination!

Have fun, and surprise your family and friends with your new skill!

How to use this book

Study each technique in turn, then knit the projects that follow. All the motifs are charted in the Motif Gallery to help you.

Techniques *These pages will help you learn the skills necessary to complete the projects.*

Step-by-step photos *Each technique is illustrated step by step.*

Projects *There are 10 projects on which you can practise your new found skills.*

Useful information *You will find all the information you need to get you started here.*

Diagrams *Each project includes a diagram to help you follow the written instructions.*

Notes *Motif references and pattern notes will guide you through the project.*

Motif Gallery *You can substitute the motifs in the projects for any of the motifs in the gallery.*

Color key *Each chart has its own instructional color key*

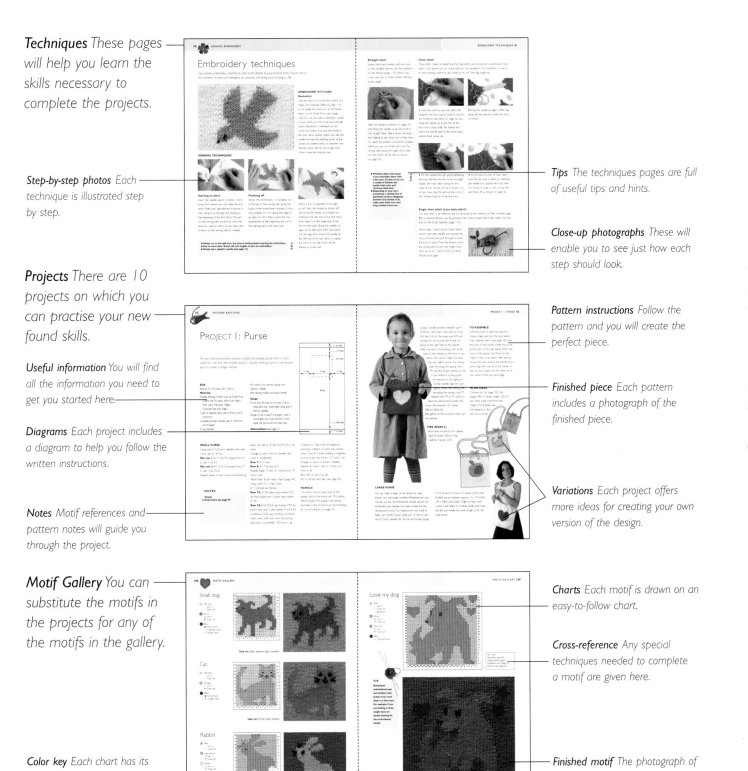

Tips *The techniques pages are full of useful tips and hints.*

Close-up photographs *These will enable you to see just how each step should look.*

Pattern instructions *Follow the pattern and you will create the perfect piece.*

Finished piece *Each pattern includes a photograph of the finished piece.*

Variations *Each project offers more ideas for creating your own version of the design.*

Charts *Each motif is drawn on an easy-to-follow chart.*

Cross-reference *Any special techniques needed to complete a motif are given here.*

Finished motif *The photograph of the finished picture will help you to visualize the motif.*

KNITTING KNOW-HOW

A quick refresher course for knitters, showing all you need to know to make any of the projects in this book, from basic knitting techniques, through assembly, to trimming with fringes and tassels.

Materials and equipment

All you need to start knitting is yarn, needles, and a few accessories. For picture knitting, the ingredients are almost the same, but some yarns are more suitable for picture knitting than others, and there are some extra accessories you will find useful.

Bulky (chunky) wool

Bulky (chunky) wool/acrylic

Aran-weight Shetland wool

Aran-weight cotton/angora

Aran-weight wool

Sport-weight cotton/acrylic

Double knitting wool/acrylic

Double knitting cotton

4-ply wool

4 ply wool

YARN

There's a wonderful range of yarns available to today's knitter, with new yarns and colors appearing every season. Choose carefully for picture knitting, following the guidelines below.

Yarns are available in many different "weights" from extra-bulky through bulky, Aran, sport, double knitting, and fingering to four-ply or even finer. The names given to these various weights can only ever be a rough guide because the terms used by different manufacturers do not always correspond.

Choosing yarns for picture knitting

For picture knitting, it is best to choose a smooth, soft yarn that is not too tightly twisted, so the different colors will "sit together" neatly. Firmly twisted yarns will highlight any slightly uneven stitches.

Yarns may be animal fibers (wool, mohair, angora, silk); vegetable (cotton, linen, ramie, bamboo); synthetic (acrylic, polyester, polyamide/nylon); or blends of these fibers. Animal fiber yarns, especially those with a high wool content, have the slight elasticity that will help your picture knitting look neat, but with practice you can use almost any yarn.

One important consideration, of course, is color—some motifs (such as animals) require particular shades, while for other motifs (such as flowers) you can vary the colors according to the yarn available. The widest color ranges are found in the most popular yarn weights: Aran, sport and double knitting.

As a rule, try to choose the same brand of yarn for all the colors in your project, unless you want to introduce a different texture (see page 62). This will ensure that all of the gauges match, and will avoid future problems with uneven shrinkage after washing.

EMBROIDERY THREADS

For embroidery on knitting, you need thread that is not too fine or fragile. If you just need a tiny amount of a color to embroider the details (such as eyes) on a motif, tapestry wool can be ideal (use it double if necessary). Tapestry wools are available in a huge range of colors, and one skein may be all you require. Other embroidery threads suitable for adding details to knitting are Pearl Cotton number 5 (medium thickness), and Soft Cotton.

YARN STORAGE

Store unused balls and oddments of yarn away from dust and dampness in transparent plastic bags or boxes, sorting them by weight, fiber content, and color. An organized collection of odd balls and remnants is a picture knitter's best friend.

TIPS

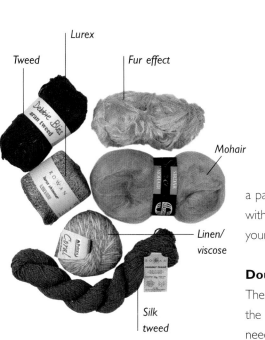

Tweed / Lurex / Fur effect / Mohair / Linen/viscose / Silk tweed

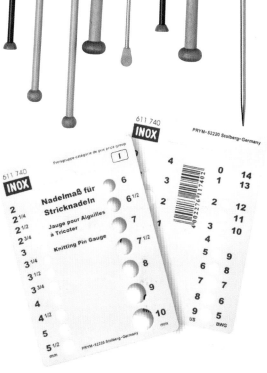

a particular project. If you like to knit with the end of one needle tucked under your arm, choose long needles.

Double-pointed needles

These are sold in sets of four or five, in the same range of sizes as pairs of needles, and in various lengths. They are pointed at both ends and are generally used for knitting in the round, and in this book for knitting I-cords (see page 32).

Needle gauge

A needle gauge is useful for checking the size of unidentified needles (such as double-pointed), and also for thrift shop bargains. Before the introduction of European sizing in millimeters (mm), UK and Canadian sizes were formerly numbered from 14 (small) to 000 (large), (the opposite way to US sizes). An heirloom collection of needles is a great find, but always check the sizes with a gauge.

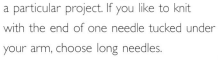

NEEDLES

The type of needles you choose (plastic, metal, bamboo, or wood) is a matter of personal preference, as is the length you choose to work with. The size (diameter) is crucial to obtaining correct gauge.

Pairs of needles

Needles may be plastic, metal (aluminum or steel), wood, or bamboo, and come in a range of different sizes (diameters) to suit different weights of yarn. They are also available in different lengths from 8 inches (20cm) to 16 inches (40cm) to suit the number of stitches required for

NEEDLE CARE
- **Needles should be kept clean and dry, stored flat with the points protected.**
- **Plastic and aluminum needles may be washed in warm water if necessary.**
- **Damaged needles will snag the yarn as you knit—replace them.**

TIPS

EQUIVALENT NEEDLE SIZES

Needles are sized in the U.S. from 0 to about 20, and in Europe from 2mm to 15mm or more. There is not an exact match between the two systems, but if you always check your gauge (see page 25) you can use either size type, as available.

US	EUROPE	US	EUROPE
0	2mm	9	5.5mm
1	2.25mm	10	6mm
3	3mm	10.5	6.5 or 7mm
4	3.25mm	11	8mm
5	3.5mm	13	9mm
6	4mm	15	10mm
7	4.5mm	17	12 or 13mm
8	5mm	20	15mm

OTHER EQUIPMENT

If you are already a knitter, you probably own most of the equipment you need. There are just one or two extras you may want to acquire along the way.

Sewing-up needles

Look for needles with large eyes and blunt tips to prevent splitting strands of yarn. They are sold as "yarn needles" or "tapestry needles," and are available in a wide range of sizes to suit any type of yarn.

Large-headed pins

Use these to hold knitted pieces together as you sew them. Large heads prevent the pins from disappearing between the stitches.

Small sharp scissors

Always use scissors for cutting yarn, never break it between your fingers.

Tape measure and ruler

Buy a new tape measure from time to time, as old ones stretch with use and become inaccurate. A ruler is useful for accurately measuring your gauge (see page 25).

Plastic bobbins

Wind small amounts of yarn onto bobbins (as on page 36) to help prevent tangles when picture knitting.

Ring markers

Rings of plastic or metal are used in this book to slip onto the needles to mark the side edges of the charted stitches. They should be smooth, not split rings, and fit loosely onto the needles, so you can slip them from one needle to the other as you knit each row. (You can substitute loops of contrast yarn, as on page 39). Don't confuse ring markers with stitch markers, which are split rings or other shapes.

Stitch markers

These are split so you can slip them into the knitting at any point, to mark a particular stitch or the ends of a particular row. In this book, they are left in place until the knitted piece is completed and used as a guide to placement when finishing. You can substitute a short length of contrast yarn tied in place.

Stitch holders

These are like huge safety pins. Use them for temporarily holding stitches, such as the neckband stitches on a sweater (see page 27).

Chart holder

Needlework shops sell magnetic chart boards, mainly for cross stitchers, but they are ideal for picture knitters, too. Color-copy your chosen chart from our Motif Gallery, hold it on the board with two of the magnetic strips and use the third strip to underline the row you are knitting.

Useful information

ABBREVIATIONS

Knitting patterns from different sources may use different abbreviations, so always read the key to any pattern before you start knitting, to make sure you understand the terms used. These are the abbreviations used in this book:

A, B, C, etc	colors used for motif charts	m1tbl	make one through back loop (see page 23)
K	knit	mm	millimeters
P	purl	cm	centimeters
K2tog	knit two together (see page 24)	yds	yards
P2tog	purl two together (see page 24)	gm	grams
ssk	slip, slip, knit (see page 23)		
P2togtbl	purl two together through back loops (see page 24)		

BRACKETS AND ASTERISKS

[ ] **Square brackets** These are used in instructions in this book to indicate figures that apply to different sizes, e.g. 1st size [2nd size, 3rd size].

( ) **Parentheses (round brackets)** These are used to indicate helpful, extra information, such as page references and metric measurements.

* **Asterisks** These may indicate a stitch sequence to be repeated, e.g. "* K1, P1, repeat from * to end" means "K1, P1, then repeat these 2 stitches in turn to the end of the row." They may also indicate a whole section of instructions to be repeated, for example "Work as Back from ** to**" means "follow the instructions for the back from the first pair of asterisks ** to the second pair **."

EQUIVALENT WEIGHTS AND MEASURES

US	UK & EUROPE
¾ ounce	20 grams
1 ounce	28 grams
1¾ ounces	50 grams
2 ounces	60 grams
3½ ounces	100 grams
1 inch	2.5 centimeters
4 inches	10 centimeters
39½ inches	1 meter
1 yard	91.5 centimeters

Basic techniques

BEGIN WITH A SLIP KNOT
Every piece of knitting begins with a slip knot.

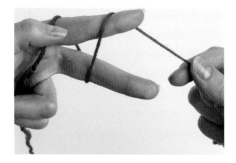

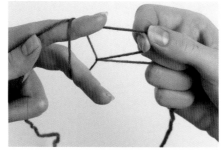

1 Unwind about 12 inches (30cm) of yarn from the ball and place the tail to your left and the ball to your right. Wind the ball end clockwise around two fingers of your left hand.

2 Pull a loop from the ball end through the loop on your fingers, from behind.

3 Slip the tip of one needle through the new loop from front to back. Tighten the knot by pulling on the tail and the ball end at the same time. This is the first stitch for any cast-on method.

HOLDING YARN AND NEEDLES
There are many ways to hold your yarn and needles, so it's up to you to use whichever method you prefer. Here are just two ways: the English method is the one used for the photographs in this book, but you may find holding the yarn in your left hand (the Continental method) more comfortable.

The English (right-hand) method

Step 1 Hold the needle with the stitches in your left hand. Your forefinger should be close to the needle tip, with the other three fingers supporting the needle. Put the little finger of your right hand behind the yarn, twist your hand to loop the yarn around your little finger, then lift the yarn with your forefinger, as shown.

Step 2 Pick up the empty needle with your right hand and hold it with your forefinger close to the tip and the other three fingers supporting the needle from below. If you are using long needles you can tuck the end of the right needle under your right arm. To wrap the yarn for a stitch, move your right forefinger forward without completely letting go of the needle.

The Continental (left-hand) method

Step 1 Hold the needle with the stitches in your right hand, with your forefinger close to the needle tip, and the other three fingers supporting the needle. Put the little finger of your left hand behind the yarn, turn your hand to loop the yarn around your little finger, then lift the yarn with your forefinger, as shown.

Step 2 Transfer the needle with the stitches to your left hand, and pick up the empty needle in your right hand. Both needles are held with the forefinger near the tip and the other three fingers underneath. Rather than wrap the yarn for a stitch, you catch it with the right needle tip, turning your hands slightly with the palms toward you.

CASTING ON

Casting on creates the stitches that form the edge of your knitting. Here are three ways to cast on, suitable for different purposes: you may want a firm, elastic edge suitable for beginning a garment piece with ribbing (method 1 or 2), or a less bulky edge with little stretch (method 3).

Method 1: Two-needle cable cast-on

This is a general purpose cast-on that forms a firm but elastic edge suitable for most purposes.

1 Make a slip knot (see page 16). Hold the needle with the knot in your left hand and the other needle in your right. Insert the tip of the right needle into the front of the loop from left to right. Wind the ball end of yarn counterclockwise around the tip of this needle, as indicated by the arrow, in the same way as for a knit stitch (see page 19).

2 Pull the new loop toward you, through the old loop.

3 Insert the tip of the left-hand needle into the new loop from right to left, and let the new loop slip off the right needle onto the left needle. Now you have two stitches on the left needle.

4 Insert the tip of the right needle under the left needle, between the stitch you just made and the one before. Wind the yarn counterclockwise around the right needle.

5 Pull the new loop through and slip it onto the left needle. Now you have three stitches on the left needle.

6 Repeat steps 4 and 5 until you have the number of stitches you need.

● If you require a firmer edge, such as when beginning a garment with garter stitch (see page 22), work the two-needle cable cast-on as given, then work the first row through the back loops of the stitches instead of the front. This tightens the stitches by twisting them.

● Sometimes a looser or less bulky edge is required, as when the edge will be sewn into a seam. To make a loose cast-on, work as above, but for each new stitch insert the point of the right-hand needle into the loop of the stitch just formed (instead of behind it), in the same way as step 1.

TIPS

Method 2: Double cast-on

This is also known as the German method, or the Long Tail cast-on.

1 Make a slip knot (see page 16), leaving a long tail at least three times the width of your knitting. So for a piece measuring 10 inches (25cm) wide, leave a tail of at least 30 inches (75cm). Put the slip knot onto a needle, held in your right hand, and arrange the long tail to the left of your left thumb, and the yarn to the ball to the right of your forefinger. Hold both ends of yarn against your left palm with your other fingers, as shown. Hold your thumb and forefinger at right angles.

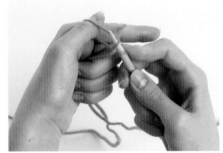

2 Use the needle tip to pick up the strand of yarn at the base of your thumb, from below.

3 Then pick up the strand in front of your forefinger, from right to left. Lift the loop of yarn on your thumb over the needle tip, so drawing a new loop through onto the needle.

4 Tighten the new stitch onto the needle. Repeat steps 2 to 4 until you have the number of stitches you need.

Method 3: Single cast-on (thumb method)

This method makes a less bulky edge, useful where the edge will be taken into a seam (see page 28). It is often used to add a small group of stitches to the side edge of knitting, as shown here (otherwise, begin with a slip knot, as above).

1 Hold the needle with the stitches on in your right hand. Hold the yarn in your left hand, looped around your thumb as shown.

2 Use the needle tip to pick up the yarn at the base of your thumb, from below.

3 Let the loop slip off your thumb onto the needle.

4 Pick up another loop of yarn with your thumb and repeat steps 2 and 3 as many times as you need.

KNIT A ROW

1 Slip the right needle tip from left to right into the first stitch on the left needle, below the left needle and in front of the yarn held in your right hand. Take care not to split the stitch with the point of the needle.

2 For the English method, use your right forefinger to carry the yarn counterclockwise around the right needle and between the two needles from left to right. (For the Continental method, catch the yarn from the right with the right needle tip.)

3 Use the right needle tip to pull the loop of yarn toward you, through the first stitch on the left needle.

4 Slip the first stitch off the left needle. One knit stitch is on the right needle.

BUTTONHOLES

Buttonholes are often worked by binding off a group of stitches on one row, (see page 21), then casting the same number on again on the next row, using the two-needle cable method (see page 17). When casting on the new stitches, before you slip the last one onto the left needle, bring the yarn between the needles, to the side of the work facing you, then transfer the last cast-on stitch to the left needle. This will tighten the stitch and make a neater buttonhole.

5 Repeat steps 2, 3, and 4. Every few stitches, push the stitches on the right needle down from the tip to prevent them bunching together in your right hand, and push the stitches on the left needle up toward the tip. When all the stitches from the left needle have been knitted onto the right needle, you have made one row of knit stitches. Swap the needle with the stitches to your left hand to begin the next row.

PURL A ROW

1 Hold the needle with the stitches in your left hand, and the empty needle in your right hand, as before. Hold the yarn in front of the right needle and insert the right needle tip into the first stitch on the left needle, from right to left, in front of the left needle.

2 Use your right forefinger to wrap the yarn counterclockwise around the right needle tip as shown. (For the Continental method, use your left forefinger to wrap the yarn counterclockwise).

3 With the right needle tip, pull the loop of yarn away from you, through the first stitch.

4 Slip the first stitch off the left needle. One purl stitch is on the right needle.

5 Repeat steps 2 to 4 until all the stitches from the left needle have been worked onto the right needle. You have made one row of purl stitches. Notice how the purl row forms a row of loops on the side of the work facing you. Swap the needle with the stitches to your left hand to begin the next row.

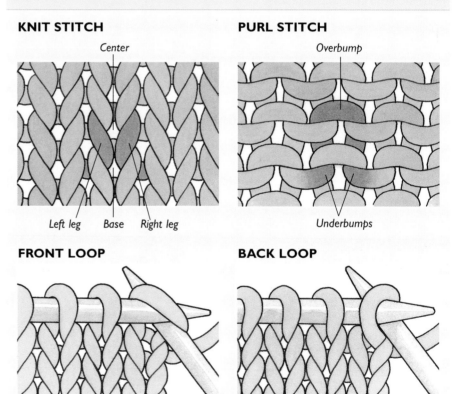

STITCH CONSTRUCTION

KNIT STITCH

Center

Left leg   Base   Right leg

PURL STITCH

Overbump

Underbumps

FRONT LOOP

BACK LOOP

When the stitches are on the needles, the "right leg" is the "front loop" of the stitch, and the "left leg" is the "back loop." Usually the right needle is inserted through the front loop of a stitch. In some special cases the needle is inserted through the back loop of a stitch.

BINDING OFF (CASTING OFF)

Binding off links stitches together at the end of a piece of knitting. You might need to bind off all the stitches, or just a certain number (for example, for an armhole shaping or a buttonhole). A bound-off edge should not be too loose or too tight. It should stretch by about the same amount as the rest of the piece. If you need a looser, more elastic edge, for example, on a neckband, change to a needle one or two sizes larger than the previous rows.

1 Knit the first two stitches in the usual way onto the right needle. Insert the tip of the left needle from left to right into the front of the first stitch you knitted.

2 Lift the first stitch over the second stitch, and off the right needle. One stitch remains on the right needle. You have bound off one stitch. Knit the next stitch. There are now two stitches on the right needle. Repeat as required.

3 When you bind off all the stitches, you will be left with one stitch on the right needle. Cut the yarn leaving a tail of at least 6 inches (15cm).

4 Wrap the tail around the right needle, lift the last stitch over it and pull the tail through to make a neat finish.

- When binding off just a few stitches, for example, to shape an armhole, count the stitches as you lift them off, not as you knit them. The stitch remaining on the right needle does not count as a bound-off stitch; it is the first stitch of the next row.
- When binding off a piece worked in rib or another textured stitch, work each stitch as knit or purl according to the pattern.

TIPS

JOINING IN A NEW BALL AT THE START OF A ROW

You will need to join in a new ball at the beginning of a row when the previous ball is used up, or when knitting stripes. To join in new colors when picture knitting, see page 39.

Tie the new yarn around the end of the old yarn with a single overhand knot, leaving a tail of at least 6 inches (15cm). Push the knot up close to the edge of the work and begin the next row with the new ball. When the piece is complete, undo the knot and run in the yarn ends (see page 29).

- When you think you have enough yarn left for TWO rows, tie a slip knot at the center of the remaining length of yarn. Work one row. If you reach the knot, untie it and complete the row, then join in a new ball. If you don't reach the knot, untie it and repeat the process.

TIPS

Basic stitches

Stockinette stitch (stocking stitch)

This is the stitch used for nearly all picture knitting. The side edges tend to curl toward the back. Work one row of knit stitches and one row of purl stitches. Repeat these two rows as required.

Reverse stockinette stitch

This is simply stockinette stitch used with the purl side as the right side of the work. It is often worked by beginning with a purl row.

Garter stitch

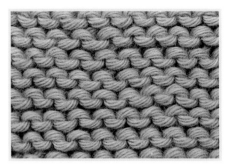

Garter stitch looks the same on both sides. It will not curl at the edges. Work one row of knit stitches. Repeat this row.

1 x 1 Rib

This is the simplest rib stitch. It will not curl at the edges and is often worked at the lower edges of garments, and for neckbands, using smaller needles than the main parts for a neat finish.
Begin with an even number of stitches:
Row 1: *Knit 1, Purl 1, repeat from * to end.
Repeat this row.

2 x 2 Rib

This rib stitch is often used in the same way as 1 x 1 rib, but it has more stretch. Begin with a number of stitches that will divide by 4 (e.g. 16, 28, 40).
Row 1: Knit 1, * Knit 2, Purl 2, repeat from * to last 3 stitches, Knit 3.
Row 2: Knit 1, *Purl 2, Knit 2, repeat from * to last 3 stitches, Purl 2, Knit 1.
Repeat these 2 rows. The knit stitch on each edge forms a garter stitch selvage.

Seed stitch

This stitch makes a knobbly texture all over. Both sides look the same, and it does not curl. Begin with an odd number of stitches:
Row 1: * Knit 1, Purl 1, repeat from * to last stitch, Knit 1.
Repeat this row. On each row, you knit the purl stitches (the ones with the little bumps facing you), and purl the knit stitches (the smooth ones facing you).

● **The edges of stockinette or reverse stockinette are often rather loose and untidy. To prevent this, work a GARTER STITCH SELVAGE: Knit the knit rows as usual, but also knit the first and last stitch of each purl row. This turns the edge stitches into garter stitches, making them tighter. The little bumps that form on each edge make it easy to match the rows when sewing seams.**

TIP

Shaping

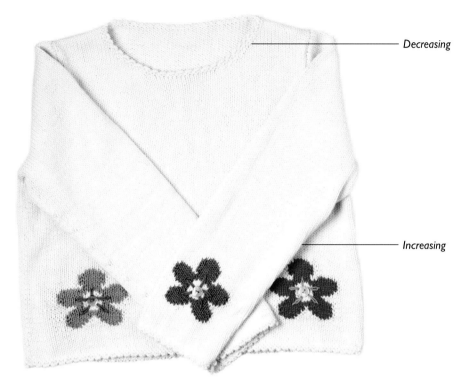

— Decreasing

— Increasing

DECREASING STITCHES

Again, there are several ways to decrease a stitch. Some methods slant to the right and others to the left, so for a neat appearance it is important to use the correct technique.

Slip, slip, knit (abbr. ssk)

This method creates a left-slanting decrease.

1 Insert the right-hand needle into one stitch on the left needle as if to knit, and slip the stitch onto the right needle. Slip the next stitch in exactly the same way.

2 Wrap the yarn around the right needle in the usual direction for a knit stitch. Slip the tip of the left needle from left to right into the two slipped stitches.

INCREASING STITCHES

There are several ways to increase a stitch (that is, to make an extra stitch), but this way is the neatest. Work the increase one stitch in from each edge of a piece such as a sleeve, or spread several increases evenly along a row where you need a sharp increase in total width (for example, after a ribbed waistband). It is usually worked on a right side row.

Invisible increase (make one through back loop) (abbr. m1tbl)

1 Knit to where you want the extra stitch to be. Hold the two needle tips slightly apart—there will be a bar of yarn between them. Slip the left needle tip underneath this bar, pulling it up to make a new loop on the left needle.

2 Now knit into the back of the new loop (see page 18): insert the right needle into the center of the new loop from right to left, wind the yarn in the usual way and form a knit stitch. Carry on knitting the row. You have made one extra stitch. It will sit neatly between two stitches, without any gaps or holes.

3 Lift the two stitches together, off the right needle.

Knit two together (abbr. K2tog)

By knitting two stitches together, you create a right-slanting decrease.

1 Insert the right needle through the fronts of two stitches on the left needle from left to right. Wrap the yarn in the usual way for a knit stitch.

2 Draw the new loop through and drop both stitches together from the left needle.

Purl two together (abbr. P2tog)

Worked on a wrong side row, this decrease also creates a right-slanting decrease on the right side of the work.

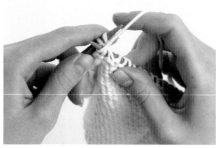

1 Insert the tip of the right needle from right to left through two stitches on the left needle.

2 Wrap the yarn in the usual way for a purl stitch.

3 Draw the new loop through, away from you, and allow both stitches to drop from the left needle.

Purl two together through back loops (abbr. P2togtbl)

Worked on a wrong side row, this method produces a left-slanting decrease on the right side of the knitting.

1 Insert the tip of the right needle from left to right through the backs of two stitches on the left needle. The right needle tip should be below the left.

2 Wrap the yarn in the usual direction for a purl stitch.

3 Pull the new loop through, away from you, and allow both stitches to drop from the left needle.

Working from patterns

Always read a knitting pattern through before you start, to make sure you understand all the abbreviations and techniques involved. If your pattern includes instructions for several sizes, it is a good idea to highlight all the figures that apply to your chosen size.

CHECK YOUR GAUGE

Correct gauge is crucial to the finished size. If your gauge is too loose, your knitting will be too big, and if your gauge is too tight, your knitting will be too small. Gauge depends on the yarn you use, the size of your needles, and also on your own knitting style: some people knit more tightly than others. Always check your own gauge and match it to the gauge quoted in the instructions, then your knitting will be the right size. Instructions usually quote a gauge like this: "x stitches and y rows to 4 inches (10cm) measured over stockinette using size z needles."

MEASURING

Measurements in this book are given in both inches and centimeters (cm). These two systems do not correspond exactly, so choose which to use and stick to it throughout the project. It is difficult to measure the width of knitting in progress (that is why correct gauge is important) but you can measure the length: Lay the work on a flat surface and use a tape measure. Measure along a vertical line of stitches at the center of the knitting.

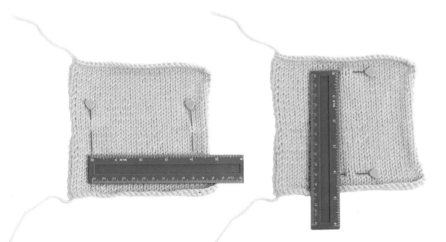

I Start with the correct yarn and needles quoted in the instructions. Cast on enough stitches for about 6 inches (15cm) width, work in stockinette for 6 inches (15cm), and bind off. Wash and dry the sample piece as described on page 29. Lay the sample flat and use a ruler to place two pins 4 inches (10cm) apart along a straight row of knitting, at the center of the piece. Count the number of stitches between the pins: 20 stitches are shown here.

2 Now do the same thing along a vertical line of stitches. There are 26 rows shown here. So the gauge for the sample shown is 20 stitches and 26 rows to 4 inches (10cm).

3 If you have fewer stitches and/or rows to 4 inches (10cm) than the gauge you need, your knitting is too loose and you should knit another sample with smaller needles, then measure again. If you have too many stitches and/or rows to 4 inches (10cm), your knitting is too tight. Make another sample with larger needles.

> ● **Sometimes gauge is measured over a particular stitch pattern, instead of over stockinette. Work your sample piece in the stitch pattern.**
> **TIP**

YARN SUBSTITUTION: BALL BANDS

If you want to use a different yarn to that quoted on a knitting pattern, you should choose a substitute that knits to the same gauge. Most yarns are labeled with a ball band, giving you all the information you need.

1 The gauge guide tells you the recommended gauge for stockinette stitch. If this matches the gauge on your knitting pattern, you can safely choose this yarn as a substitute.

2 The recommended needle size may differ from your knitting pattern. Working one or two gauge samples as described on page 25, will tell you which needles are right for you.

3 Match the yarn content as closely as you can. If the yarn content doesn't match, you may need extra yarn.

4 Some yarns (such as cottons) are heavier than others, so 50gm of a cotton yarn may be several yards (meters) shorter than 50gm of wool. If your knitting pattern quotes a length for the recommended yarn, you can compare the length for your substitute to calculate how many balls to buy.

> ● If possible, buy just one ball of a substitute yarn and check your gauge before buying all the yarn for a project.
> ● When buying several balls of one color, make sure they all have the same dye lot number. The slightest color variation between dye lots can show up as a stripe across your knitting.
>
> **TIP**

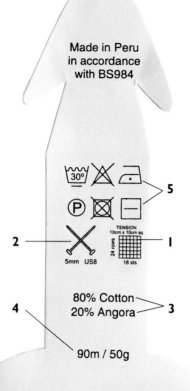

Made in Peru
in accordance
with BS984

5

TENSION
10cm x 10cm sq
24 rows
18 sts
5mm   US8

2

1

80% Cotton
20% Angora

3

4

90m / 50g

Debbie Bliss

cotton angora

Colour:
15508

Dyelot:
12

6

5 The care instructions on the ball band will enable you to look after your knitwear.

6 If more than one ball of yarn is required to create your finished piece, make sure that you purchase yarn with the same color and dye lot number.

Assembly techniques

PICKING UP STITCHES

This technique is used when knitting neckbands and borders. Stitches may be picked up from a side edge, a bound-off edge, or a cast-on edge, and further rows worked, avoiding the need for a seam.

On a side edge

1 With right side of work facing, hold one needle in your right hand and insert the tip one whole stitch in from a side edge. Pass the yarn around the needle tip in the usual direction for a knit stitch.

2 Draw the new loop through the edge, making one stitch on the needle.

3 Repeat steps 1 and 2 as required along a side edge. Be sure to pick up the correct number of stitches, spacing them evenly.

 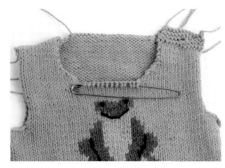

On a bound-off edge

On a bound-off edge, insert the needle through the center of each stitch and work as steps 2 and 3. (On a cast-on edge, insert the needle between the stitches).

Stitches left on a holder

At the center front of this sweater, stitches have been left on a holder without binding them off. Sometimes you can open up the holder and knit the stitches directly from it, but often the holder is the wrong way round: slip the stitches from the holder onto a double-pointed needle of a suitable size, then knit them in the usual way.

Baby sweater, page 80

TO ASSEMBLE

Finishing neatly can make or break your project. Most knitting books recommend pressing your knitted pieces before finishing. However, picture knits always benefit from washing (see page 29), which helps even out the stitches, and this is best done after joining the pieces together.

Use the same yarn as you used for the knitting, (if the knitting yarn is bulky, substitute a matching, finer yarn with the same fiber content). Choose a blunt-tipped needle (a tapestry needle or yarn needle, as page 14) with a large eye that easily takes the yarn.

Mattress stitch (invisible seam) on side edges

This is the neatest and most useful seam for most knitted projects. It is usual to work this seam one whole stitch in from each edge as shown. The sewing yarn here is a contrast color so you can see how it works, but you can often begin a seam with the tail from casting on. If not, begin by leaving a 4-inch (10-cm) tail and run it in later.

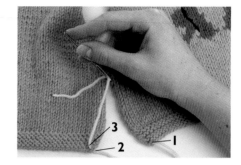

1 Lay the two edges to be joined side by side on a flat surface, right side up and with the lower edges toward you. Bring the needle through to the right side at 1 on the right edge, then through the left edge from 2 to 3.

2 Bring the needle through the right edge again in exactly the same place, making a figure eight.

3 Pull the figure eight quite tightly. Then take the needle through the left edge again from 2 to 3. Pull through.

4 Insert the needle at 1 (where it last came out) on the right edge, and bring it out at 4, one row above, so the needle passes under just one bar of yarn. Pull through.

5 Insert the needle on the left edge, where it last came out, and bring it out one row above. Pull through. Repeat steps 4 and 5 when joining garter stitch or reverse stockinette.

6 When joining stockinette, pick up two bars with each stitch.

7 Draw the edges gently together as you sew. Even when worked with a contrasting yarn, as here, the seam is almost invisible.

Mattress stitch on other edges

Sometimes you need to join a cast-on or bound-off edge of one piece to the side edge of another piece. The number of stitches on one edge will never match the number of rows on the other.

I Use large-headed pins to hold the pieces together. Work from right to left. Begin by leaving a 4-inch (10-cm) tail to run in later.

2 Work one stitch in from the side edge of one piece, and through the loops of the last row of stitches on the other piece. On the bound-off edge, make one stitch into the center of each stitch of the last row as shown.

3 The stitches into the side edge may pick up one or two bars, as required to keep the work flat. The needle here is making a stitch under one bar, but the previous stitch is under two bars. Try to spread the stitches evenly along the seam.

RUNNING IN YARN ENDS

The tails left at the side edges of a piece of knitting may be used for sewing seams if they are long enough. Shorter tails should be run in along a seam. After you have sewn a seam, run in all the tails like this: Simply run the needle through the edges of the stitches for about 2 inches (5cm), pull through and snip off the excess. If you have two tails attached at the same point, run one up the seam and the other down to avoid excess bulk.

BLOCKING PICTURE KNITS

The easiest way to block a picture knit is to wash it. This will help to even out the stitches. You will need lukewarm water, detergent suitable for woolens and delicate fabrics, and two towels.

I Add a little suitable detergent to lukewarm water. Handle the knitting gently, squeezing the water through it for a couple of minutes.

2 Support the whole weight when you lift the knitting out of the water. Rinse thoroughly in two or three changes of water. Lay the knitting out on a towel, roll up the towel and squeeze it to draw out as much water as possible. Then lay the knitting flat on another, dry towel and pat it to shape. Leave it to dry completely.

Finishing touches

Add fringes, tassels, cords, or pompons for that final flourish. Here are some simple techniques that require only small amounts of yarn.

FRINGES

You will need a piece of cardboard, a pair of scissors, and a crochet hook.

1 Decide on the depth of fringe you require. Cut a piece of card about ½ inch (1.2cm) wider than this measurement. Each separate tail of a fringe usually needs at least two strands of yarn. Wind the yarn around the card as many times as required for the number of separate tails you need.

2 Cut through all the strands along one edge of the card. You now have lots of strands, all more than twice as long as the depth of your fringe.

3 With right side of knitting facing, insert the crochet hook from wrong side to right side where you want the first tail to be. Fold two (or more) strands of yarn in half and catch the loop with the hook.

4 Pull the loop through the knitting.

5 Catch the free ends with the hook, and pull them through the loop on the hook. Pull on the free ends to tighten the knot.

6 Repeat as required. Trim all the free ends to the same length.

Scarf, page 44

TASSELS

You will need a piece of cardboard, scissors, and a tapestry needle.

1 Decide how long you want the tassel to be. Cut a piece of card about ½ inch (1.2cm) wider than this measurement. Wind the yarn around the card as many times as you want.

2 Cut the yarn leaving a tail of about 10 inches (25cm) and thread this tail into the needle.

3 Slip the yarn off the card and wind the tail tightly around it, about ½ inch (1.2cm) from one end. Bind tightly with several turns.

4 Slip the needle underneath the turns and bring it out at the top.

5 Pass the needle through all the small loops at the top of the tassel.

6 Knot the tail tightly at the top of the loop. Don't cut it off.

7 Cut through all the strands at the bottom of the tassel. If they are not quite even, trim them straight.

8 Use the yarn tail to sew the tassel in place.

Hat, page 46

I-CORD

This cord is a knitted tube, useful for ties and handles. You will need two double-pointed needles, two or three sizes smaller than the size recommended for your yarn.

1 Cast on 3, 4, or 5 stitches (no more). Knit one row in the usual way.

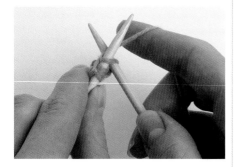

2 Without turning the work around, pass the needle with the stitches to your left hand. Push the stitches along to the right end of the needle. Pass the yarn across the back of the stitches and pull it tight to bunch the stitches together, then use the empty needle to knit another row from right to left.

3 Repeat to the length required. The knitting forms a small tube.

BRAIDS

We have used simple braids to add tails to some of our animal motifs. You can also use them for ties or purse straps. You will need a large safety pin.

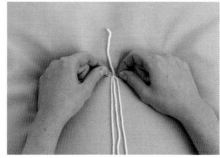

1 Decide how long you want the braid to be. Cut one length of yarn, at least half as long again as this measurement, plus 4 inches (10cm). Cut a second length twice as long as the first and knot it around the first length, about 4 inches (10cm) from one end. Pin the knot to a firm surface such as your ironing board or the back of a chair.

2 Braid the three strands in the same way as you would braid hair: pass the left strand over the central one, then the right strand over the central one, and repeat as required.

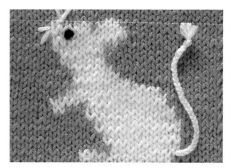

3 When you reach the length you want, tie an overhand knot with all three strands and snip the ends close to the knot.

4 Use the 4-inch (10-cm) tail at the top to sew the braid in place.

4 Bind off. Pull gently on the finished cord to close the gap where the yarn passes across the back.

Purse, page 42

POMPONS

Use pompons to decorate hats and other accessories, or add a pompon tail
to our Rabbit motif (page 108). You can buy plastic pompon makers in various sizes,
or you can use cardboard and scissors to make any size you need. You will also
need a pair of drawing compasses and a tapestry needle.

1 Use compasses to draw two circles on
the card, the same size as you want for
your pompon. Draw a smaller circle,
about half the size, at the center of each.
Cut out the circles and the central holes.

2 Place the two circles together and
wind the yarn round and round passing it
through the center, to cover all the
cardboard evenly. You can use several
colors if you wish.

3 When the hole at the center gets
smaller, thread the yarn into the tapestry
needle and carry on winding until the
hole is full.

4 Part the strands on the edge of the
circles and insert the tip of the scissors
between the two layers of card. Cut
through all the strands around the edge
of the circles.

5 Pull the card circles apart and tie a
strand of yarn tightly around the center.
Leave a tail of about 8 inches (20cm) to
sew on the pompon.

6 Cut away the card circles and fluff up
the pompon.

7 Snip untidy ends from the
completed pompon.

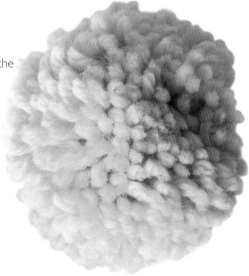

PICTURE KNITTING

From reading a chart to running in the yarn tails, here's the insider knowledge you need to make your picture knits look really professional.

Knitting from charts

The golden rule for picture knitting is to use a separate ball of yarn for each separate area of color. Your work will then lie flat, without puckering.

READING A CHART

Each square on a chart represents one stitch of your knitting. Charts in this book are drawn on a rectangular grid (to represent the typical gauge of stockinette stitch), but charts are sometimes drawn on a square grid, so we'll call them squares.

The chart shows the right side of the knitting. For stockinette stitch, you knit the right side rows, which are numbered on the right with odd numbers (1, 3, 5, and so on), and purl the wrong side rows, numbered on the left with even numbers (2, 4, 6, and so on). The row number is placed at the beginning of each row. The arrows remind you that right side rows (odd numbers) are read from right to left, and wrong side rows (even numbers) are read from left to right.

The symbol △ shows you where to join a new ball.

The symbol ▼ shows you where to finish off a ball. The colors of the symbols correspond with the suggested colors for the motif.

YARN PREPARATION

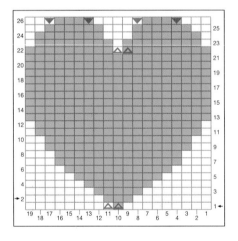

How many balls?

Before you start to knit your motif, study the chart to see how many balls of each color are required. On charts in this book, the symbol △ shows you where to join in a new color (and the symbol ▼ shows you where to finish off a color). So if you count up the △ symbols in each color, you'll know how many balls of each color you need. The chart assumes you are already knitting with the background color A (cream), so you will begin the first row (at bottom right of the chart) with the ball you are already using. On the Small Heart chart, you will need two balls of B: one beginning at the lower point of the heart on row 1, and then another smaller ball to join in on row 22. You will also need two more balls of A: one to knit the stitches to the left of the heart (beginning on row 1), and another small ball to join in on row 22 for the central stitches at the top of the heart.

WINDING BALLS AND BOBBINS

Wind small amounts of yarn onto bobbins. Wind larger amounts into center-pull balls (see next page). This helps to keep the colors from tangling as you knit. You can buy various shapes and sizes of bobbins suitable for holding small amounts of yarn. Wind yarn onto bobbins, as shown opposite, slipping the tail through the slit to prevent unwinding.

You can also cut your own bobbins from cardboard. Use tracing paper to copy this shape onto cardboard and cut it out. You can enlarge or reduce the shape by photocopying, to suit different thicknesses and amounts of yarn.

How much yarn?

If your whole project requires several balls of A to complete, you can simply start another ball or two of A and use up the remainders later. If you need to divide one ball into several small balls, you can estimate like this: Count the number of stitches on the chart area, for example, at the top of the Heart, the central background area in A contains 13 stitches, counted backward and forward across the area, between △ and ▼.

1 Wind the yarn around your needle (not too tightly), once for each stitch. Unwind it and add a further 10 or 20 percent. Then add 8 inches (20cm) for a 4-inch (10-cm) tail at each end.

2 Cut the yarn and wind it onto a bobbin (or into a small ball). The remainder of the ball can be joined in for a larger area.

TIPS

● **To estimate yarn required for larger areas, count the chart squares, then wind the yarn 10 times round the needle and measure it. This length will knit about 10 stitches, so you can figure out how much yarn you need. Always be generous when estimating, it's so annoying to run out of a color on the last few stitches!**

● **If you can, always unwind a ball of yarn from the center: that way, it won't roll around and tangle with other balls as you knit.**

WINDING A CENTER-PULL BALL

Step 1 Hold a 12-inch (30-cm) tail of yarn under three fingers, open out your thumb and forefinger, and wind in a figure eight around them, about 15 or 20 times.

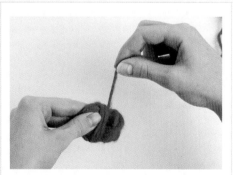

Step 2 Slip the yarn off your fingers and fold it in half, keeping your thumb over the top of the tail, where it enters the ball. Wind another 10 or 15 turns over both the ball and two fingers, so the winding is not too tight.

Step 3 Continue winding quite loosely, changing direction every 10 turns or so, always keeping your thumb over the top of the tail. Tuck the end of the yarn under the last few turns to hold it in place. Pull on the starting tail to unwind from the center.

JOINING A NEW BALL
On a knit row

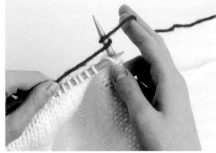

1 To join in a new ball (B), insert the right needle tip into the next stitch in the usual way, and lay a 4-inch (10-cm) tail of B across the right needle tip, with the ball of B to the right and the tail to the left.

2 Take the yarn from the ball counter-clockwise around the right needle tip.

FINISHING OFF A BALL
When it's time to finish with the ball you're using, cut the yarn leaving a 4-inch (10-cm) tail. This will be dealt with later, along with all the other tails. (It's always neater to cut yarn rather than break it with your fingers).

On some of our charts, you may think you still need that color, but if you look you'll find another ball of the same color is still attached somewhere close by, and that's the one to use.

3 Flip the tail away from you, across the yarn leading to the ball.

4 Pull the new loop toward you through the loop on both needles, knitting the stitch in the usual way. The little twist formed by flipping the tail helps to hold the new yarn in place.

On a purl row

1 Insert the right needle tip into the next stitch in the usual way for a purl stitch, and take the yarn from the ball clockwise around the right needle tip: that is, in the opposite direction to the usual purl stitch.

2 Flip the tail toward you, across the yarn leading to the ball.

3 Pull the new loop away from you through the loop on both needles to purl the stitch in the usual way. Again, the little twist formed by flipping the tail helps to hold the stitch in place.

KNIT CHART ROW I

Motifs may be placed anywhere on the knitting. Placing ring markers at either side of the charted stitches will help you count correctly from the chart.
Use small plastic rings (which should fit loosely over your needles), or make your own markers by tying little loops of contrasting yarn.

I Using A, work to the row where the motif will begin, ending with a wrong side row. Using A, knit the stitches to the right of the chart area. Slip a marker onto the right-hand needle, to mark the right edge of the stitches on the chart.

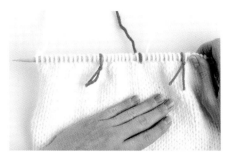

2 Now knit chart row I from right to left. Join in each color as shown on page 38. Slip a second marker onto the right needle to mark the left edge of the charted stitches. Knit with the second ball of A to the end of the row.

PURL CHART ROW 2: CHANGE COLORS ON PURL ROW

On the following rows, you slip the markers and at each color change, cross the yarns to prevent holes between the colors.

I Chart row 2 is a purl row. With the second ball of A, purl to the first marker you come to. Slip the marker from the left needle onto the right.

2 Read Heart chart row 2 from left to right. When colors change, leave A dangling and pick up B from the right of A, so the two colors cross. This is a purl side color change.

KNIT CHART ROW 3: CHANGE COLORS ON KNIT ROW

On a knit row, the colors must again be crossed on the wrong side.

I Use A to knit to the first marker and slip it. Read Heart chart row 3 from right to left. When colors change, pick up B from the right, beneath A, so the two colors cross. This is a knit side color change.

3 Pull B gently and use it to purl to the next color change. Leave B dangling and pick up the next ball of A, making another purl side color change.

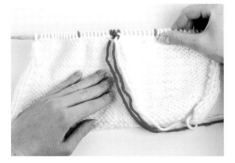

4 Pull A gently to tighten the last stitch it was used for, and purl to the next marker. Slip the marker as before and use A to purl to the end of the row.

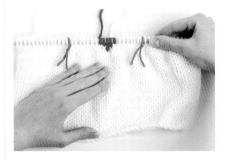

2 Tighten B gently, and complete the row, changing colors as step I and slipping the second marker.

COMPLETE THE PICTURE

Continue reading from successive chart rows, joining new balls, finishing off colors and always remembering to cross the yarns over when changing colors. When the motif is complete, carry on knitting in the usual way to finish the piece. Don't worry if the stitches look loose. The appearance will improve when you run in the ends (it is easier to do this later when the work is off the needles). Washing the work (see page 29) helps even out stitches, too.

RUNNING IN TAILS

When you have finished the piece of knitting, you need to run all the little tails in on the wrong side. You can neaten uneven stitches at the same time. You will need a tapestry needle (see page 14) to suit your yarn.

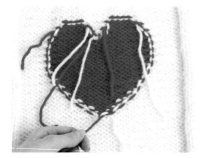

1 On the wrong side, pull gently on all the little tails to tighten the first and last stitches of each area, so they are the same size as the other stitches.

2 Stitches often look uneven at either side of a color change. On the right side, use a large tapestry needle to pull gently on the "leg" of a tight stitch (the leg right next to the color change), to pull a little extra length from the looser stitch above or below. When you wash your finished project, the stitches will even out some more.

3 On the wrong side, thread a tail into the tapestry needle. Weave it in and out of the loops where the colors change, along the edge of an area of color for at least 1 inch (2.5cm), (2 inches [5cm] for bulky or slippery yarns).

4 Pull the tail through and snip off the excess.

5 Do the same with all the other tails. You can weave along the top or bottom of an area of color, or along the sides.

WHEN TO FLOAT

Rules are made to be broken. Sometimes it does make sense to carry a color across the wrong side of the work!.

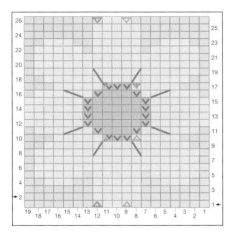

This chart is marked with just one Δ symbol in color A (green), on the first row, meaning that all the stitches right of the flower are worked with the ball of A you have to start with, and all the stitches left of the flower with another ball of A.

All the stitches in B (pink) are also worked with just one ball. So on chart rows 4 and 5 (and rows 22 and 23), you should carry the colors across the wrong side from one area to the next. This forms strands across the wrong side, called "floats."

It's fine to make a float across as many as five stitches, but only for one or two rows. If you float across the same group of stitches for several rows the knitting will pucker up. Only make floats where you need a color for just a few more stitches, on one or two rows. If you joined in new balls for these few stitches, you would have lots of tails and not enough space to run them in (see page 40).

1 To float A behind B on a wrong side (purl) row, purl the first group of stitches in A, leave A dangling, pick up B (don't forget to cross the yarns at the back) and purl the first group of stitches in B.

2 Leave B dangling and pick up A again, from behind B as if you were crossing the two yarns. Spread out the B stitches so they are not bunched together, and purl the next group of stitches with A. Pick up B again if required for further stitches.

3 Work floats on a knit row in a similar way. Form the floats on the wrong side of the work (away from you). Always leave the yarns dangling on the wrong side, and always cross them at the back of the work.

4 This is the wrong side of the Cosmos motif, up to row 6, showing the floats of both rows 4 and 5. The floats should not be too tight or the knitting will be puckered, but neither should they be too loose, or the stitches will be uneven.

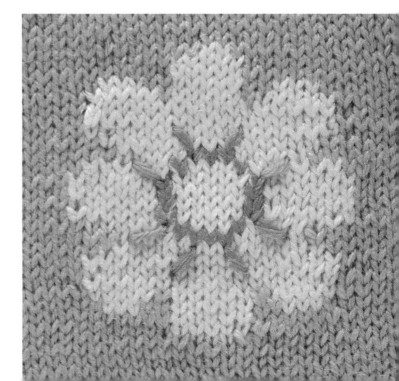

PROJECT 1: Purse

For your first picture knit project, choose this simple purse with a Heart motif. You can knit the smaller purse in double knitting yarn, or use heavier yarn to make a larger version.

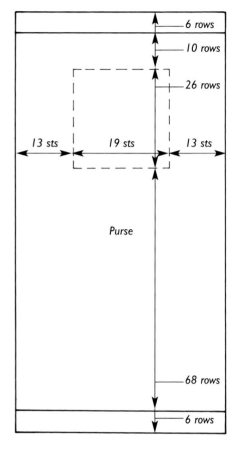

6 rows

10 rows

26 rows

13 sts   19 sts   13 sts

Purse

68 rows

6 rows

SIZE

Approx. 8 x 8 inches (20 x 20cm)

Materials

Double Knitting Cotton such as Sirdar Pure
Cotton DK 93 yards (85m) per 50gm:
   Main color: Mid-pink 100gm
   Contrast: Pale pink 20gm
1 pair of needles each size 6 (4mm) and 4
   (3.25mm)
2 double-pointed needles size 4 (3.25mm),
   short length
2 ring markers

40 inches (1m) narrow piping cord
Tapestry needle
Pink sewing thread and sharp needle

Gauge

22 sts and 30 rows to 4 inches (10cm)
   measured over stockinette using size 6
   (4mm) needles.
Gauge is not crucial if a change in size is
   acceptable, but if your tension is too
   loose the purse will not look neat.

Abbreviations see page 15

SMALL PURSE

Using size 4 (3.25mm) needles and main color, cast on 44 sts.

Rib row 1: K1, * K2, P2, repeat from * to last 3 sts, K3.

Rib row 2: K1, * P2, K2, repeat from * to last 3 sts, P2, K1.

Repeat these 2 rows, twice more, knitting

NOTES

Charts
● **Small heart, see page 94**

twice into last st of last row. 45 sts. 6 rib rows.

Change to size 6 (4mm) needles and work in stockinette:

Row 7: K to end.

Row 8: K1, P to last st, K1.

Repeat these 2 rows, 33 more times. 74 rows in all.

Work from Small Heart chart (page 94), using colors A = main color,

B = contrast, as follows:

Row 75: K13A, place ring marker, K19 sts from chart row 1, place ring marker, K13A.

Row 76: K1A, P12A, slip marker, P19 sts from chart row 2, slip marker, P12A, K1A.

Continue in this way, working successive chart rows until chart row 26 (wrong side row) is complete. 100 rows in all.

Continue in main color throughout, removing markers on next row: repeat rows 7 and 8, 5 times, knitting 2 together at end of last row. 44 sts. 110 rows in all.

Change to size 4 (3.25mm) needles.

Repeat rib rows 1 and 2, 3 times. 116 rows in all.

Bind off in K and P as set.

Run in all the yarn tails (see page 40).

HANDLE

Tie a knot close to each end of the piping cord, so the knots are 35½ inches (90cm) apart. This piping cord will be enclosed in the I-cord as you knit. Knitting an I-cord is shown on page 32.

Using 2 double-pointed needles size 4 (3.25mm) and main color, cast on 4 sts. Knit the 4 sts in the usual way. Without turning the work, push the 4 new sts along to the right end of the needle. Hold one end of the piping cord at the back of the knitting so the knot is just below the cast-on edge, and take the yarn tightly across the wrong side, enclosing the piping cord. ** Use the empty needle to knit 1 row. Without turning, push the stitches to the right end of the needle. Take the yarn tightly across the wrong side enclosing the piping cord. ** Repeat from ** to ** until you reach the second knot, when the I-cord will measure 35½ inches (90cm). Bind off.

Pull gently on the I-cord to even out the stitches.

TIES (MAKE 2)

Work two I-cords as for Handle, each 8 inches (20cm) long (without piping cord).

TO ASSEMBLE

Fold the purse in half, matching the ribbed edges, and join the side seams with mattress stitch (see page 28). Sew the ends of the handle inside the purse, at the tops of the side seams. Stitch the ends of the piping cord firmly to the inside of the purse seams with sewing thread. This will prevent the handle from stretching. Sew one tie at the center of the top front edge, and the other tie at the center of the top back edge.

MORE IDEAS

Choose the Lily (page 99), Cat (page 108), or Apple (page 106), or any other small motif from the Gallery. The finished size will depend on the yarn you choose.

LARGE PURSE

You can make a larger purse simply by using thicker yarn and larger needles. Whatever yarn you choose, use the recommended needle size for the stockinette and needles two sizes smaller for the ribbing and I-cords. Our large purse was made in bulky yarn (Sirdar Nova) using size 10 (6mm) and size 8 (5mm) needles. At the recommended gauge of 12 sts and 16 rows to 4 inches (10cm), the finished purse measures approx. 15 × 15 inches (38 × 38cm), and used 150gm of main color (cream) and 30gm of contrast (pink). We made the ties and handle the same length as for the small purse.

PROJECTS 2 and 3:
Scarf and hat

This cozy scarf in Aran-weight yarn is quick and easy to knit. The matching pull-on hat has a shaped crown for a neat fit. Make a set for each member of the family!

SIZE

Width: 8¼ inches (21cm)

Length, excluding fringe: 47½ inches (120.5cm)

Materials

Aran-weight yarn such as Jamieson and Smith Soft Spun wool approx. 87½ yards (80m) per 50gm:

Main color: Blue 150gm

Contrast: Orange 50gm

1 pair of needles each size 6 (4mm) and size 8 (5mm) (or size to obtain correct gauge)

2 ring markers

Tapestry needle

Medium crochet hook

Gauge

19 sts and 24 rows to 4 inches (10cm) measured over stockinette using size 8 (5mm) needles.

Gauge is not crucial provided a change in size is acceptable. However, if your gauge is too tight the scarf will be less flexible, and if it is too loose extra yarn may be required.

Abbreviations see page 15

SCARF

Using size 6 (4mm) needles and main color (blue), cast on 39 sts.

Rib row 1: * K1, P1, repeat from * to last st, K1.

Rib row 2: *P1, K1, repeat from * to last st, P1.

Repeat these 2 rows twice more. 6 rib rows.

Change to size 8 (5mm) needles. Work in stockinette:

Row 1: K to end.

Row 2: K1, P to last st, K1.

Repeat these 2 rows, 5 more times. 18 rows in all.

Place motif

* Follow the Small Star chart on page 96, using colors as follows: A = main color (blue), B = contrast color (orange).

Row 13: K10A, place ring marker, K19 sts from chart row 1, place ring marker, K10A.

Row 14: K1A, P9A, slip marker, P19 sts from chart row 2, slip marker, P9A, K1A.

NOTES

Charts
- Small star, see page 96

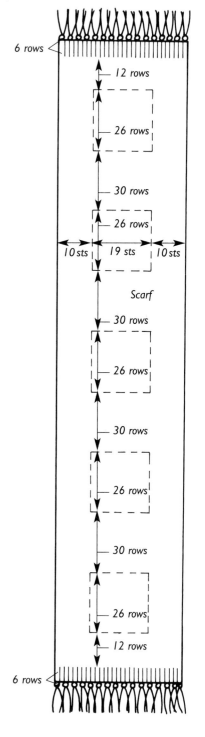

Continue in this way, working
successive chart rows until
chart row 26 (wrong side row)
is complete. 44 rows.
Change to main color (blue).
Removing markers on next
row, repeat rows 1 and 2, 15
times. * 74 rows.
Repeat 56 rows from * to *,
three more times. 242 rows.
Work 26 chart rows once again.
268 rows. 5 motifs are
complete.
Repeat rows 1 and 2, 6 times in
all. 280 rows.
Change to size 6 (4mm)
needles.
Repeat rib rows 1 and 2, 3
times in all. 286 rows.
Bind off in K and P to
match rib.

TO ASSEMBLE

Run in all yarn tails. Make a fringe at each end as follows:
See page 30. Use a piece of card 4 inches (10cm) wide to wind and cut 76 x 8 inch (20cm) lengths of blue. Use 2 lengths for each knot of fringe, attaching with crochet hook to every alternate stitch of cast-on and bound-off edges. Trim fringe to 3 inches (7.5cm).

SIZES

To fit head:

18–19	20–21	22–23	inches
46–48	51–53	56–58	cm

Actual measurement:

18	20	22	inches
46	51	56	cm

Materials

Aran-weight yarn such as Jamieson and Smith Soft Spun wool approx. 87½ yards (80m) per 50gm:
Main color: Blue 100gm (for all sizes)
Contrast: Orange 10gm (for all sizes)
1 pair of needles each size 6 (4mm) and 8 (5mm) (or size to obtain correct gauge)
5 ring markers
Tapestry needle

Gauge

19 sts and 24 rows to 4 inches (10cm) measured over stockinette using size 8 (5mm) needles.
Check your gauge as on page 25. Correct gauge is important for correct sizing.

Abbreviations see page 15

NOTES

- Figures in square brackets [ ] refer to the two larger sizes. Where only one figure is given this refers to all sizes.

- Charts
- Small star, see page 96

HAT

Using size 6 (4mm) needles and main color (blue), cast on 86 [96, 106] sts.
Rib row 1: * K1, P1, repeat from * to end.
Repeat this row 17 [19, 21] more times, purling into front and back of last stitch of last row. 87 [97, 107] sts. 18 [20, 22] rib rows.
Change to size 8 (5mm) needles. Work in stockinette:
Row 1: K to end.
Row 2: K1, P to last st, K1.
Repeat these 2 rows 0 [1, 2] more times. 20 [24, 28] rows in all.

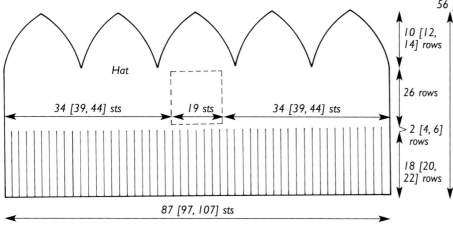

56 [62, 68] rows

Hat

34 [39, 44] sts

19 sts

34 [39, 44] sts

87 [97, 107] sts

10 [12, 14] rows

26 rows

2 [4, 6] rows

18 [20, 22] rows

Place motif

Follow the Small star chart on page 96, using colors as follows: A = main color (blue), B = contrast (orange).

Next row: K34 [39, 44]A, place ring marker, K19 sts from chart row 1, place ring marker, K34 [39, 44]A.

Following row: K1A, P33 [38, 43]A, slip marker, P19 sts from chart row 2, slip marker, P33 [38, 43]A, K1A.

Continue in this way, working successive chart rows until chart row 26 (wrong side row) is complete, removing markers on last row. 46 [50, 54] rows.

Continue in main color (blue) throughout

Shape crown

Crown row 1: K1, place ring marker, * K2tog, K13 [15, 17], ssk, place ring marker, repeat from * 4 more times, K1. 77 [87, 97] sts.

Crown row 2: K1, P to last st slipping each marker, K1.

Crown row 3: K1, slip marker, * K2tog, K to 2 sts before marker, ssk, slip marker, repeat from * 4 more times, K1. 67 [77, 87] sts.

Crown row 4: K1, P to last st slipping each marker, K1.

Repeat Crown rows 3 and 4, 1 [2, 3] more times. 57 sts.

Next row: As Crown row 3.

Following row: K1, slip marker, * P2tog tbl, P to 2 sts before marker, P2tog, slip marker, repeat from * 4 more times, K1. 37 sts.

Repeat last 2 rows once more. 17 sts.

Last row: K1, remove marker, * slip 1, K2tog, pass slip st over, remove marker, repeat from * 4 more times, K1. 7 sts. Cut yarn leaving an 8-inch (20cm) tail. Use tapestry needle to thread tail through remaining 7 sts, pull up tightly and secure.

TO ASSEMBLE

Run in all yarn tails. Join center back seam, using mattress stitch (see page 28), reversing seam on lower half of rib to allow for turn back. Make a tassel as follows:

See page 31. Use a piece of card 4 inches wide to make a tassel with approx. 16 x 8 inch (20cm) lengths of blue. Sew tassel to top of hat.

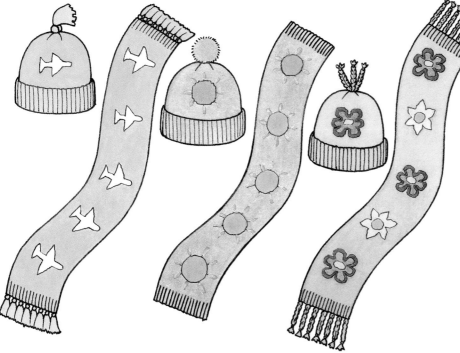

MORE IDEAS

Use any small motif from the Gallery on the hat, but for the scarf choose a motif that "reads" when seen upside down as the scarf is worn. You could choose the Plane (page 118), or Small Sun (page 96). Several of the flowers are suitable, such as the Peony (page 101), Cosmos (page 99), Daisy (page 102) or Daffodil (page 101), so you could knit the scarf with two (or more) different flowers. You can trim the hat with a pompon (page 33) or a little bunch of braids (page 32).

ADDING EMBROIDERY

Embroidery stitches, beads, and sequins can all be used to add details to picture knits, or to decorate larger areas, for that personal touch that makes a design your own.

Embroidery techniques

Use simple embroidery stitches to add small details to your picture knits. Flower stems and centers, or eyes and whiskers on animals, will bring your knitting to life.

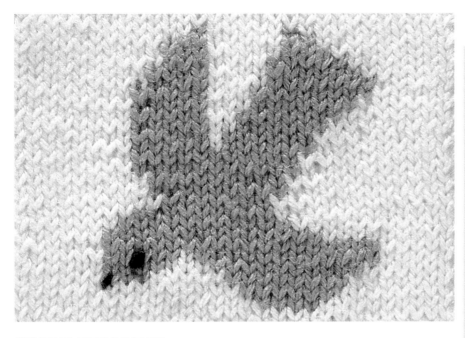

GENERAL TECHNIQUES

EMBROIDERY STITCHES
Backstitch

Use this stitch to smooth the outline of a shape (for example, Balloons, page 116), or for single fine lines such as the flower stems on the Small Posy chart (page 102). You can also add a backstitch outline to any motif, as in the Small star example below. Backstitch is indicated on our charts by broken lines, and the breaks in the lines show exactly where you take the needle through the knitting: either at the center of a knitted stitch, or between two stitches. Some stitches are longer than others, especially sloping ones.

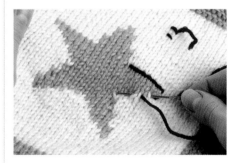

Starting to stitch

Insert the needle about 4 inches (10cm) away from where you will make the first stitch. Make two backstitches to secure it, then bring it up through the knitting at the beginning of the first stitch. The yarn on the wrong side should not cross the area you want to stitch, or you may catch it down on the wrong side by mistake.

Finishing off

When the embroidery is complete, run in the tail on the wrong side, along the backs of the embroidery stitches. (If this is not possible, run it in along the edge of an area of color). Then unpick the two backstitches at the beginning and run in the starting tail in the same way.

Work a line of backstitch from right to left. Start the thread as shown left and bring the needle up through the knitting at the left end of the first stitch, then insert it at the beginning of the line (to the right). Bring the needle up again at the left end of the next stitch. Pull through, then insert the needle at the left end of the last stitch to repeat the stitch to the left. Finish off the thread as shown left.

● **Always run in the tails from the picture knitting before starting the embroidery.**
● **Use no more than 18-inch (45-cm) lengths of yarn for embroidery.**
● **Always use a tapestry needle (see page 14).**

TIPS

Straight stitch

Some charts are marked with just one or two straight stitches, like the whiskers on the Mouse (page 110). These may cross over two or three knitted stitches at any angle.

Start the thread as shown on page 50 and bring the needle up at one end of the straight stitch. Take it down through the knitting at the other end of the stitch. To reach the position of another straight stitch, you can run in the yarn (on the wrong side) along the edge of an area of color. Finish off the tails as shown on page 50.

TIPS

- **Whiskers often look better if you embroider them with a fine yarn. It's easy to try out a couple of stitches and decide what color and thickness looks best.**
- **Depending on your yarn, sometimes a vertical line of backstitch tends to disappear between the stitches. If so, make each stitch two rows long, instead of one row.**

Chain stitch

Chain stitch makes a bolder line than backstitch, and is ideal for curved lines. Chain stitch is not shown on our charts, but you can substitute it for backstitch or use it to add a strong outline to any motif, as on our Tote Bag (page 66).

1 Hold the work so you can stitch the required line from top to bottom. Secure the thread as described on page 50, and bring the needle up at the top of the line. Form a loop with the thread and insert the needle back in the same place, where it last came out.

2 Bring the needle up again a little way along the required line, inside the loop of thread.

3 Pull the needle through, gently tightening the loop. Stitches should not be too tight. Repeat the chain stitch along the line. Make all the stitches the same length: one or two rows long for vertical lines, one or two stitches long for horizontal lines.

4 At the end of a line of chain stitch, hold the last loop in place by inserting the needle just outside the loop. Take the thread through to the wrong side and finish off, as shown on page 50.

Single chain stitch (Lazy daisy stitch)

This easy stitch is an effective way to decorate flower centers, (as Teen Sweater, page 88) or several stitches may be grouped into a daisy shape. We've also used it for the tusk on the Small Elephant (page 110).

Work steps 1 and 2 as for Chain Stitch above. Insert the needle just outside the loop of thread and pull through to hold the loop in place. Float the thread across the wrong side to the next single chain stitch by up to 1 inch (2.5cm), or finish off and start again.

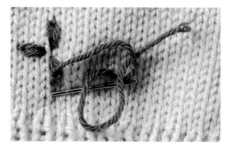

French knots

French knots make perfect little eyes for animals, birds, and fish. Our motifs also use them for fruit on the Tree (page 107), and for flower centers on the Flowerpot (page 104). The symbol for a French knot is a dot in the suggested color, positioned at the center of a knitted stitch.

1 Start the thread as shown on page 50 and bring the needle up at the base of the required stitch (that's at the center of the stitch below the dot). Hold the thread between your thumb and forefinger and twist it twice (or maybe three times, but no more) around the needle tip.

2 Insert the needle at the center of the stitch marked with the dot. Hold the thread taut with your thumb, to keep the coils in place, as you push the needle down. Then pull the needle through from below, keeping the coils close together.

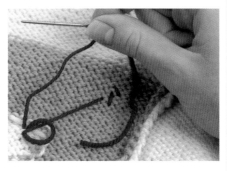

3 The finished knot should be quite tight and close to the surface.

4 Make a tiny backstitch on the wrong side, behind the knot. Finish off both tails as described on page 50.

Duplicate stitch

This embroidery stitch duplicates the shape of stitches on the right side of stockinette. It is used in this book to add small details or fine lines, where joining in small balls of yarn would be untidy and tricky to handle. Worked correctly, each duplicate stitch exactly covers the stitch below. Do not stitch too tightly. Duplicate stitches are shown on our charts by a symbol in the suggested color.

1 Secure the thread as shown on page 50. The easiest direction for duplicate stitch is along a row of knitting from right to left. Bring the needle up at the base of the first stitch to be covered. Pass the needle from right to left under both "legs" of the stitch above the one you are covering.

2 Insert the needle back through the knitting at the base of the first stitch, where it first came out. Pull through gently. The duplicate stitch should exactly cover the stitch below, the duplicate thread following the same track as the yarn of the knitted stitch. Bring the needle up again at the base of the next stitch to the left and repeat as required.

3 To work up a line of stitches from bottom to top, duplicate the lowest stitch of the line as before, then bring the needle out at the center of this stitch to begin the stitch above.

4 You can also work a line of stitches from left to right: bring the needle up at the base of the left-hand stitch and pass it from left to right under both "legs" of the stitch above, then back down again at the base of the first stitch. Repeat to the right.

5 To work down a line of stitches, first duplicate the stitch at the top of the line. Bring the needle out at the base of the next stitch below, then pass it from right to left under both "legs" of the duplicate stitch above, (not the knitted stitch). Take the needle back down through the base of the stitch and bring it out one row below to begin the next stitch down.

BEADS AND SEQUINS

You can use beads, sequins, charms, and buttons to add an extra touch that brings a design to life.

Sewing on sequins

A sequin may be firmly attached by stitching a small bead at the center, so the thread is not visible.

Sewing on beads

Beads, buttons, and charms should be firmly sewn in place with matching sewing thread. If they are widely spaced, fasten off the thread securely after each bead, and begin again for the next.

1 Instead of a French knot, sew on a bead for an eye or flower center. Use sewing thread to match the bead and a small, sharp needle that fits easily through the bead. Secure the thread with two backstitches on the wrong side of the knitting, just behind where the bead will be. Bring the needle through to the right side, thread on a bead, and take the needle through to the back of the work.

2 Repeat this stitch two or three times, then fasten off the thread with another backstitch behind the bead. If you require another bead close by, within 1 inch (2.5cm) or so, you can "float" the thread across to the next position and make another backstitch before sewing on the next bead.

1 Secure the thread as for a bead, and bring the needle up through the knitting where required. Thread on the sequin, then a small bead, then take the needle down again through the center of the sequin. Repeat this stitch, pulling firmly.

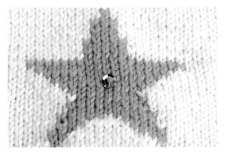

2 Secure the thread on the wrong side as for a bead.

PROJECT 4: Four-panel cushion

*Adding just a little embroidery brings to life the flower motifs used for this
cheerful cushion. Make it in soft, bright colors to suit your room.*

SIZE
To fit pillow form 16 x 16 inches
    (40 x 40cm)

Materials
Double Knitting Wool such as Paton's
    Diploma Gold DK approx. 131 yds
    (120m) per 50gm:
    Main color: Mid-pink 150gm
    1st contrast: White 75gm
    2nd contrast: Lilac 25gm
    3rd contrast: Purple 25gm
    4th contrast: Dark pink 25gm
    5th contrast: Lime 10gm
3 large buttons to fit buttonholes

1 pair of needles each size 6 (4mm)
    (or size to obtain correct gauge) and
    size 4 (3.25mm)
2 ring markers
4 stitch markers
Tapestry needle

Gauge
22 sts and 30 rows to 4 inches (10cm)
    measured over stockinette using
    size 6 (4mm) needles.
Gauge is not crucial if a change in size is
    acceptable, but if your gauge is too
    loose the cushion will not look neat
    and extra yarn may be required.

Abbreviations see page 15

side row) is complete. 36 rows.
Continue in A throughout, removing
markers on next row: repeat rows 1 and
2, 5 times in all. 46 rows in all.
Bind off.
Run in all the yarn tails and use tapestry
needle to work embroidery as chart.

SECOND SQUARE
Knit as First Square, working from Small
Rose chart (page 101), using colors
A = 1st contrast (white), B = main color
(mid-pink), C = 4th contrast (dark pink).

THIRD SQUARE
Knit as First Square, working from Lily
chart (page 99), using colors A = 1st
contrast (white), B = 4th contrast (dark
pink), C = 5th contrast (lime).

FIRST SQUARE
Using size 6 (4mm) needles and 1st
contrast (white) cast on 35 sts.
Row 1: K
Row 2: K1, P to last st, K1.
Repeat these 2 rows, 4 more times. 10
rows.
Work from Cosmos chart (page 99),
using colors A = 1st contrast (white),
B = 2nd contrast (lilac), C = 5th contrast
(lime), D = 3rd contrast (purple):

NOTES

Charts
● **Cosmos, see page 99**
● **Lily, see page 99**
● **Pansy, see page 99**
● **Small rose, see page 101**

Row 11: K8A, place ring marker, K19 sts
from chart row 1, place ring marker, K8A.
Row 12: K1A, P7A, slip marker, P19 sts
from chart row 2, slip marker, P7A, K1A.
Continue in this way, working successive
chart rows until chart row 26 (wrong

FOURTH SQUARE
Knit as First Square, working from Pansy
chart (page 99), using colors A = 1st
contrast (white), B = 2nd contrast (lilac),
C = 3rd contrast (purple), D = 5th
contrast (lime).

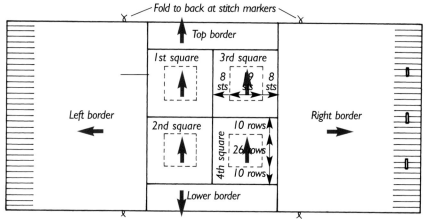

■ *Red arrows indicate the direction of working*

TOP BORDER

Using tapestry needle, 1st contrast (white) and mattress stitch (see page 28), join the four squares together to match the photograph.

With right side of work facing, using size 6 (4mm) needles and main color (mid-pink), pick up and knit 34 sts from top edge of Second Square and 34 sts from top edge of First Square (that is, 1 st from each st along top edge, omitting the 2 sts taken into the center seam). 68 sts.

Work in reversed stockinette stitch:

Row 1 (wrong side row): K to end.
Row 2: K1, P to last st, K1.
Repeat these 2 rows, 7 more times. 16 rows.
Bind off.

LOWER BORDER

Work to match Top Border, picking up sts from lower edges of Third and Fourth Squares.

RIGHT BORDER

With right side of work facing, using size 6 (4mm) needles and main color (mid-pink), pick up and knit 11 sts from right edge of Lower Border, 34 sts from right edge of Fourth Square, 34 sts from right edge of Second Square and 11 sts from right edge of Top Border. 90 sts.

Work in reversed stockinette stitch as for Top Border for 16 rows, ending right side (P) row.

Placing a stitch marker at each end of next row, continue in reversed stockinette stitch for a further 53 rows, ending wrong side (K) row.

Change to size 4 (3.25mm) needles.

Rib row 1: * K1, P1, repeat from * to end.

Repeat this row 5 more times. 6 rib rows.

Buttonhole row: Rib 20 sts as set, * bind off next 4 sts in K and P as set, 1 st on right-hand needle, rib next 18 sts,

repeat from * once more, bind off next 4 sts, rib as set to end. 3 buttonholes made.

Following row: Rib as set, casting on 4 sts over each buttonhole.

Repeat Rib row 1, 6 more times. 14 rib rows in all.

Bind off in K and P as set.

LEFT BORDER

Work to match Right Border, omitting buttonholes. Pick up sts from left edges of Top Border, First Square, Third Square, and Lower Border.

TO ASSEMBLE

Using tapestry needle and main color (mid-pink), embroider a line of chain stitch (see page 51) along the vertical seam at the center of the panel, and a second line along the horizontal seam. Fold the Left and Right Borders to the back along the marked rows so the rib rows overlap at center back, with the buttonholes on top. Join the top and bottom edges. Sew on buttons to match buttonholes. Insert pillow form.

MORE IDEAS

You could choose just one small motif from the Gallery (such as the Small Tulip, page 102) and make this cushion with four panels the same. Or choose two

motifs (such as the Small posy, page 102 and Bee, page 112). Or choose four different motifs (such as the Kite, page 116, Small Ted, page 116, Boat, page 118 and Balloons, page 116) to make a bright cushion for a child's room. Choose the contrast colors carefully for a balanced appearance.

PROJECT 5: Baby blanket

Show off your picture knitting skills by making this cuddly blanket as a gift for a new baby.

SIZE

Approx. 27 x 35 inches (67 x 87cm)

Materials

Aran-weight yarn such as Patons
  Diploma Gold Aran approx. 90 yds
  (82m) per 50gm:
  Main color: Blue 400gm
  Contrast: Cream 350gm
1 pair of needles each size 7 (4.5mm)
  (or size to obtain correct gauge)
  and 5 (3.5mm)
2 ring markers
Tapestry needle

Gauge

19 sts and 25 rows to 4 inches
  (10cm) measured over stockinette
  using size 7 (4.5mm) needles.
Gauge is not crucial if a change in size
  is acceptable, but if your gauge is
  too loose the blanket will not
  look neat, and extra yarn may
  be required.

Abbreviations see page 15

NOTES

  Charts
  ● **Moon, see page 96**
  ● **Small star, see page 96**
  ● **Mouse, see page 110**
  ● **Bird, see page 112**

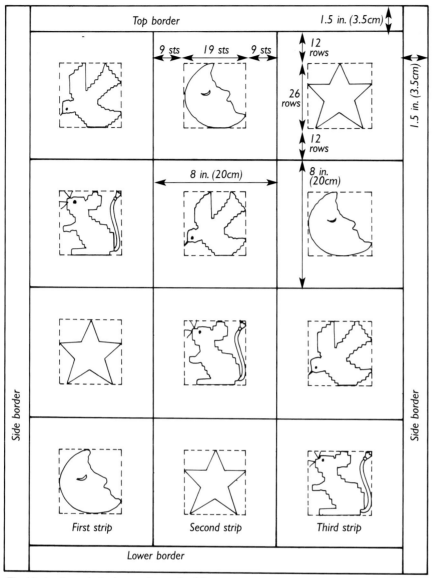

Top border   1.5 in. (3.5cm)

9 sts   19 sts   9 sts

12 rows

26 rows

12 rows

1.5 in. (3.5cm)

8 in. (20cm)   8 in. (20cm)

Side border   Side border

First strip   Second strip   Third strip

Lower border

The blanket is made in three strips, each of four squares.

FIRST STRIP

Using size 7 (4.5mm) needles and main color (blue), cast on 37 sts.

Moon square

Work in stockinette:

Row 1: K to end.

Row 2: K1, P to last st, K1.

Repeat these 2 rows, 5 more times. 12 rows.

Work from Moon chart (page 96), using colors A = main color (blue), B = contrast (cream), as follows:

Row 11: K9A, place ring marker, K19 sts from chart row 1, place ring marker, K9A.

Row 12: K1A, P8A, slip marker, P19 sts from chart row 2, slip marker, P8A, K1A. Continue in this way, working successive chart rows until chart row 26 (wrong side row) is complete. 38 rows in all. Change to main color (blue). Removing markers on next row, repeat rows 1 and 2, 6 times. 50 rows in all.

Star square

Change to contrast (cream). Repeat rows 1 and 2 as for Moon Square, 6 times in all. Work 26 rows from Small star chart (page 96) in same way as for Moon, using A = contrast (cream), B = main color (blue).

Change to main color (blue). Removing markers on next row, repeat rows 1 and 2, 6 times. 100 rows in all.

Mouse square

Work as Moon Square, but following Mouse chart (page 110), using colors A = main color (blue), B = contrast (cream). 150 rows in all.

Bird square

Work as Star Square, but following Bird chart (page 112), using colors A = contrast (cream), B = main color (blue). 200 rows in all.

Bind off in contrast (cream).

SECOND STRIP

Using size 7 (4.5mm) needles and contrast (cream), cast on 37 sts. Work Star Square, Mouse Square, Bird Square, and Moon Square all as above. Bind off in main color (blue).

THIRD STRIP

Using size 7 (4.5mm) needles and main color (blue), cast on 37 sts. Work Mouse Square, Bird Square, Moon Square and Star Square all as above. Bind off in contrast (cream).

TOP BORDER

Run in all the yarn tails. Join the strips in order from left to right with mattress stitch (see page 28), matching the squares carefully and taking 1 stitch from each edge into seams.

Using size 5 (3.5mm) needles and main color (blue), with right side of work facing, pick up and knit 36 sts from top edge of Third Strip, 35 sts from Second Strip and 36 sts from First Strip. 107 sts. Work in garter stitch:

Row 1: Slip 1 purlwise, K to end. Repeat this row 14 more times. 15 garter stitch rows.

Bind off.

LOWER BORDER

Work to match Top Border.

SIDE BORDERS (make 2)

Using size 5 (3.5mm) needles and blue, with right side of work facing, pick up and knit 7 sts from side edge of border, 140 sts from side edge of strip (i.e. 35 sts from side edge of each of 4 squares) and 7 sts from side edge of border. 154 sts. Work 15 rows garter stitch as for Top Border.
Bind off.

TO ASSEMBLE

Run in remaining yarn tails. Use main color (blue) to embroider eyes on Moons and Mice and beaks on Birds. Use contrast (cream) to embroider eyes on Birds and to make 2-inch (5cm) braid tails for Mice, as on page 32. Wash the finished blanket as described on page 29, or press, following instructions on ball bands.

MORE IDEAS

You can choose any combination of small motifs from the Motif Gallery to make your own version of the blanket: the Small Dog (page 108), Small Elephant (page 110), Cat (page 108) and Rabbit (page 108), perhaps, or the Small Ted (page 116), Double Heart (page 94), Duck (page 110) and Boat (page 118).

ADDING TEXTURE

Add another dimension to
your picture knits
by learning how to choose
suitable textured yarns,
and how to incorporate
textured stitches.

Texture techniques

There are two ways to add texture to your picture knitting. You can introduce textured yarns such as mohair, fluffy angora, multi-color tweed, sparkling lurex, fuzzy "eyelash," or fur effects. Or you can work parts of the design in textured stitches, such as seed stitch.

COMBINING DIFFERENT YARNS

The golden rule here is to choose yarns that will knit to the same gauge.

First choose your main or background yarn. If you are making one of our projects, or adapting an existing knitting pattern, choose the main yarn to match the recommended gauge, and check your own gauge as shown on page 25. If gauge is not quite so crucial (such as a scarf or cushion), choose your background yarn and match your gauge to the recommended gauge on the ball band. Then select textured or novelty yarns you would like to use. If possible, choose yarns with similar recommended gauges and washing requirements.

Test the gauge

Begin by testing the gauge of all your chosen yarns, together in one swatch.
1 Use the main yarn (blue shown here) and your chosen needles to cast on enough stitches for about 2 inches (5cm) width. Then cast on the same number of stitches in each of your contrast yarns. Here 8 stitches in each yarn are shown.

Work several rows in stockinette, keeping each group of stitches in the same color (changing colors as page 39), and cast off.
2 Check the effect. If a yarn is too thick, like the turquoise, furry yarn shown here, the stitches will be too big and the knitting will feel heavy and thick. The only thing to do is to substitute another,

finer yarn. If a yarn is too thin, like the pink chenille here, the knitting will look gappy and uneven. You need to substitute a heavier yarn.

TEXTURED YARNS

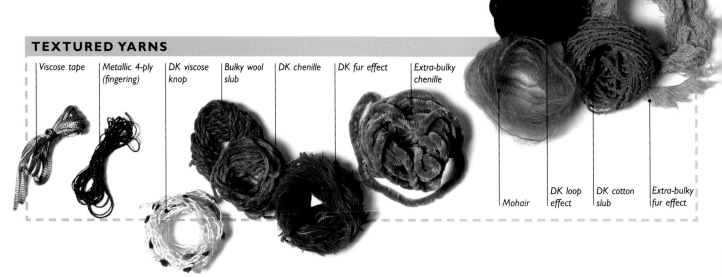

Viscose tape | Metallic 4-ply (fingering) | DK viscose knop | Bulky wool slub | DK chenille | DK fur effect | Extra-bulky chenille

Mohair | DK loop effect | DK cotton slub | Extra-bulky fur effect

A *Two strands of pink chenille wound together*

B *Pink chenille wound with fur-effect yarn*

D *Pink chenille wound with mohair*

C *Pink chenille wound with lurex*

3 If you need a heavier yarn try combining two (or more) yarns together: Wind small balls of several yarn combinations.
A: Two strands of pink chenille wound together.
B: Pink chenille wound with fur effect yarn.
C: Pink chenille wound with lurex.
D: Pink chenille wound with mohair.

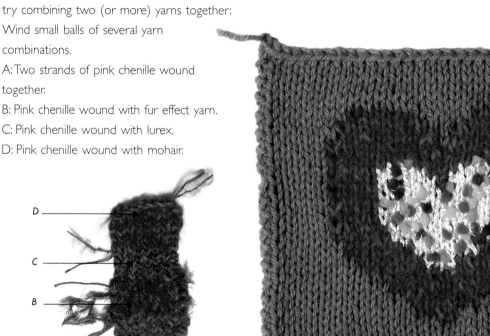

D

C

B

A

4 Using the same needles as before, knit a striped swatch a few stitches wide to test the effect of your yarn combinations: here, the double chenille (A) and the chenille plus fur (B) are too thick. The chenille plus lurex (C) is not quite thick enough, but the chenille plus mohair (D) is just right.

5 Knit another swatch as step 1 to make sure all the gauges match. The multi-color knop yarn is used double as a substitute for the heavy, turquoise yarn. The pink chenille is wound with mohair. Both gauges now match the blue main yarn.

6 You can now go ahead and knit your project. This Double Heart motif from page 94 is knitted in a combination of plain and textured yarns.

TIP

- Don't buy all the yarns for a large item until you have checked all the gauges together.
- Firm, smooth, or slippery yarns are best combined with woolly or furry ones, so the two blend together rather than separating as you knit.
- For a vibrant color effect, wind together two yarns in slightly different shades.

USING TEXTURED STITCHES

Suitable stitches for texture need to be similar in gauge to stockinette. Reverse stockinette (see page 22) is ideal, and so is seed stitch (see page 22).

Rib stitches (see page 22) tend to have more stitches and fewer rows to the inch than stockinette, while garter stitch (see page 22) tends to have fewer stitches and more rows to the inch. These stitches should be used with caution: use them for quite small areas, or for less elastic yarns like cotton, or for articles such as cushions where the knitting will be stretched by the filling. Otherwise these stitches will tend to distort the proportions of your picture.

All these stitches achieve texture by combining knit and purl stitches in different ways. You can easily add them to an existing chart.

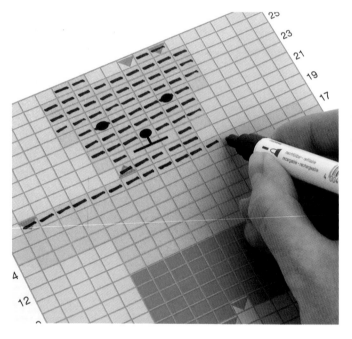

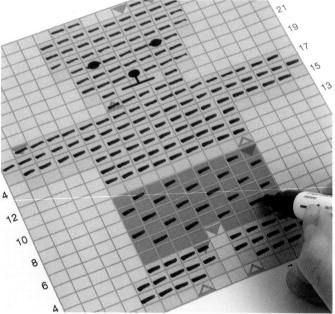

1 Photocopy the chart for the motif you want. Suppose you want to knit the teddy's body in reverse stockinette. A purl bump on the right side of the work is usually represented by a horizontal line across the chart square. Reverse stockinette is purl on right side rows and knit on wrong side rows, so all the bumps are on the right side of the work. Take care where the colors change. If you work reverse stockinette in a different color to the stitch below, the result is not a clean break between the colors: the line is broken by the overbumps of the old color. Therefore, where a stitch is a different color to the one below it, you need to work it in stockinette. Draw a line across every chart square that will be reverse stockinette.

2 Suppose you want to knit the teddy's shorts in seed stitch. Draw a line across every square that will be a purl bump on the right side of the work. Again, allow for color changes, as above.

3 When you knit from your new chart, remember that every square with a bar means "purl on a right side row, or knit on a wrong side row."

reverse stockinette

stockinette

seed stitch

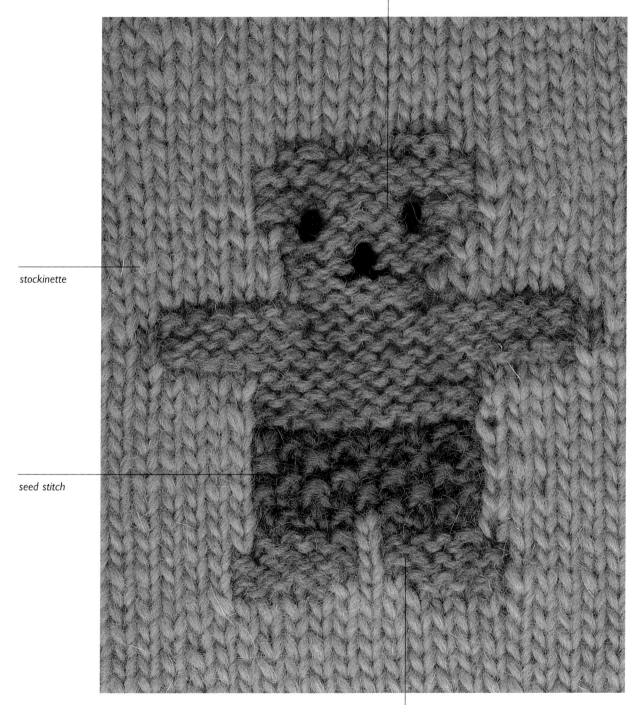

reverse stockinette

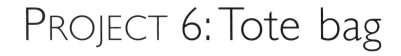

PROJECT 6: Tote bag

Add another dimension to your knitted pictures by introducing yarns of different textures. This tote bag is ideal for carrying your knitting around, and even more practical if you line it with cotton fabric.

SIZE
Approx. 14 × 12 inches (35 × 30cm) excluding handles

Materials
Aran-weight tweed yarn, such as Rowan Summer Tweed approx. 118 yds (108m) per 50gms:
  Main color: Lilac 150gm
Equivalent plain cotton yarn, such as Rowan All Seasons Cotton:
  1st contrast: White 50gm
  2nd contrast: Lime 20gm
Double knitting weight yarn for embroidery:
  3rd contrast: Orange 20gm
1 pair of needles each size 7 (4.5mm) (or size to obtain correct gauge) and 6 (4mm)
Pair of bag handles with 7-inch (17.5cm) slots
Tapestry needle
2 ring markers

4 stitch markers
Cotton lining fabric approx. 30 × 15 inches (75 × 37.5cm), optional
Sewing thread to match fabric, and sharp needle

Gauge
17 sts and 25 rows to 4 inches (10cm) measured over stockinette using size 7 (4.5mm) needles and main color. This is tighter than the recommended gauge on the ball band, but should help prevent the bag from stretching.
Gauge is not crucial if a change in size is acceptable, but if your tension is too loose the tote will not look neat, and may not fit the bag handles. Check the gauge of two different yarn types together as shown on page 62.

Abbreviations see page 15

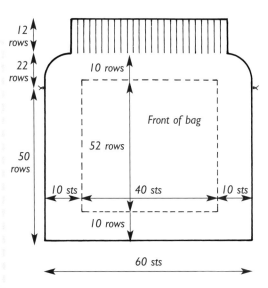

FRONT
Using size 7 (4.5mm) needles and main color (lilac), cast on 60 sts.
Row 1: K to end.
Row 2: K1, P to last st, K1.
Repeat these 2 rows, 4 more times. 10 rows in all.
Work from Large Butterfly chart (page

NOTES
Charts
• **Large butterfly, see page 113**

113), using colors A = main color (lilac), B = 1st contrast (white), C = 2nd contrast (lime) as follows:
Row 11: K10A, place ring marker, K40 sts from chart row 1, place ring marker, K10A.
Row 12: K1A, P9A, slip marker, P40 sts from chart row 2, slip marker, P9A, K1A. Continue in this way, working successive chart rows until chart row 40 (wrong side row) is complete. Placing a stitch marker at each end next row, work chart rows 41–52. 62 rows in all. Continue in main color throughout: removing ring markers on next row, repeat rows 1 and 2, 5 times. 72 rows in all.

** Change to size 6 (4mm) needles.
Dec row: K1, * ssk, K1, P2, repeat from * to last 4 sts, ssk, K2. 48 sts.
Rib row 2: K1, *P2, K2, repeat from * to last 3 sts, P2, K1.
Rib row 3: K1, * K2, P2, repeat from * to last 3 sts, K3.
Repeat rib rows 2 and 3, 4 more times, and rib row 2 once again. 84 rows in all, ending wrong side row.
Bind off in K and P as set.

BACK
Using size 7 (4.5mm) needles and main color (lilac), cast on 60 sts.
Row 1: K to end.
Row 2: K1, P to last st, K1.
Repeat these 2 rows, 24 more times. 50 rows in all.
Placing a stitch marker at each end next row, work a further 22 rows. 72 rows in all.
Complete as Front from ** to end.

TO ASSEMBLE

Run in all the yarn tails. Use the tapestry needle to work embroidery on the Front. We used 3rd contrast (orange) for the feelers as shown on the chart (in backstitch and French knots), then added a chain stitch outline (as on page 51) all around the wings and body. Join Front to Back at lower edge with matching yarn, then join the two side seams up to the stitch markers. Wash the work as described on page 29.

If you want to line the bag as shown here, do this next (see page 69).

ATTACHING HANDLES

Slip the bound-off edge of the back through the slot in one handle, and stitch the bound-off edge to the wrong side of the first rib row. Attach the other handle to the Front in the same way.

MORE IDEAS

You can use any large motif from the Gallery on this tote, such as the Large Sun motif (page 97), or Large Roses (page 100). On the Tree (page 107), you could substitute beads for the French knots.

OPTIONAL LINING Assemble and insert the lining before attaching the bag handles. Measure the bag. Add 1 inch (2.5cm) to the width only, and cut two pieces of lining fabric to this size, for example, if the bag measures 14 x 13 inches (35 x 32.5cm), cut lining pieces 15 x 13 inches (37.5 x 32.5cm). These sizes include a seam allowance of ½ inch (12mm) on the base and sides, more at the top edge.

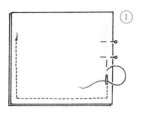

1 Pin the two pieces with right sides together and use matching sewing thread and sharp needle to backstitch around three sides as shown, so the side seams (excluding seam allowance) match the length of the side seams on the outer bag, up to the stitch markers. You can machine stitch these seams if you prefer.

2 Press all seam allowances back onto wrong side of lining, all around three sides, including the side seams left unstitched.

3 Slip the lining inside the outer bag, matching the side seams, and pin the folded edges of the lining just inside the edge of the knitting at each open side seam. On Front and Back, fold the top edge of the lining to the inside to match the last row of stockinette. Use matching thread and sharp

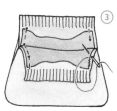

needle to slip stitch the lining in place to the side edges only.

4 On the Back, use sewing thread double to run a line of gathering stitches close to the top folded edge of the lining. Gather up the top edge to match the width of the bag and pin it in place, arranging the gathers evenly. Then backstitch the lining in place, sliding the needle through the knitting beneath so the stitches will not show through to the right side. The backstitches do not need to form a continuous line. Pull out the gathering thread. Attach the top edge of the lining to the Front in the same way. Now attach the handles as described left.

PROJECT 7: One-panel cushion

Yarns and stitches add texture, while simple embroidery, beads, and sequins make the Elephant into an exotic beast, perfect for this luxurious cushion.

SIZE

To fit pillow form: 14 x 14 inches (35 x 35cm)

Materials

Tweedy Aran-weight yarn such as Debbie Bliss Aran
   Tweed 109 yds (100m) per 50gm:
   Main color: Pink tweed 250gm balls
Plain Aran-weight yarn such as Debbie Bliss Merino
   Aran 85½ yds (78m) per 50gm:
   1st contrast: Pale pink 50gm
   2nd contrast: Gray 30gm
   3rd contrast: Blue 20gm
   4th contrast: Bright pink 10gm
   5th contrast: White, scrap of for tusk
Optional: fine Lurex filament such as Madeira
   Glissen Gloss Rainbow (wind together with 4th
   contrast before commencing): Bright pink, 1 card
   38 yds (35m)
Embroidery thread such as Pearl Cotton no. 5:
   Pink
Blue sequins
Small pink beads
1 black bead for eye
Pink sewing thread to match beads
1 pair of needles each size 7 (4.5mm) (or size to
   obtain correct gauge) and 6 (4mm)
2 double-pointed needles size 6 (4mm)
2 ring markers
Tapestry needle
Sewing needle to fit through beads

Gauge

20 sts and 28 rows to 4 inches (10cm) measured
   over stockinette stitch using size 7 (4.5mm)
   needles. Gauge is not crucial provided a change
   in size is acceptable. However, if your knitting is
   too loose the cushion will not look neat and
   extra yarn may be required.

Abbreviations see page 15

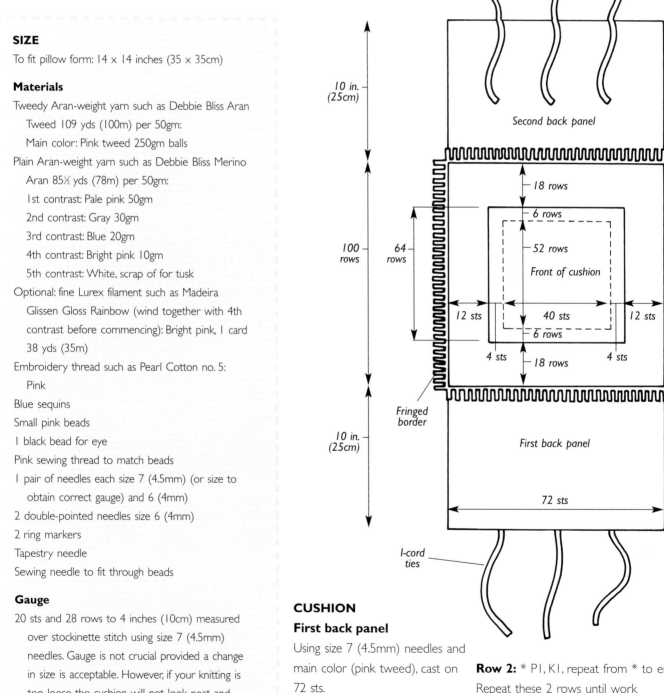

CUSHION
First back panel

Using size 7 (4.5mm) needles and main color (pink tweed), cast on 72 sts.
Work in seed stitch:
Row 1 (right side): * K1, P1, repeat from * to end.

Row 2: * P1, K1, repeat from * to end. Repeat these 2 rows until work measures 10 inches (25cm) ending right side row.

Fold line row: K to end.

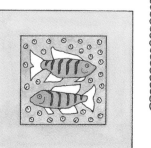

MORE IDEAS

Any large motif from the Gallery will suit this cushion, such as the Large Tulips (page 103), Large Fish (page 115) or Flowerpot (page 104). You could add silvery sequins to the Fish, or use beads for the flower centers on the Flowerpot (and add extra embroidery, or textured stitches, to the pot itself). You could omit the Fringed Border entirely, or substitute the Loop Border from Project 10.

A Pale pink
  △ Join in
  ▽ Finish off
  ╱ Backstitch

B Gray
  △ Join in
  ▽ Finish off
  ✕ Attach braid tail 2 inches (5cm) long

C Blue
  △ Join in
  ▽ Finish off

D Bright pink with lurex
  △ Join in
  ▽ Finish off

E White
  △ Join in
  ▽ Finish off

● Sew on black bead for eye

— Reverse stitch (purl on right side row, knit on wrong side row)

⣿ Sew on blue sequin with a pink bead

✛ Four single chain stitches, plus five pink beads

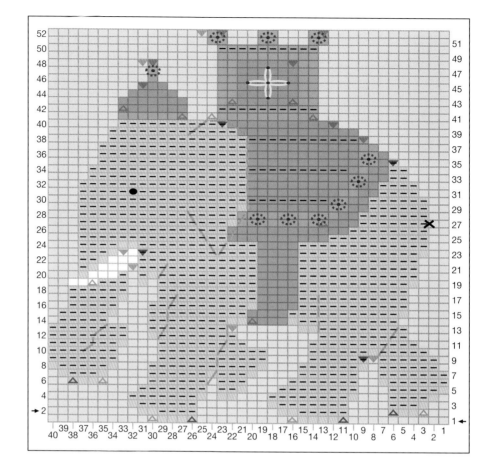

Front

Repeat rows 1 and 2, 9 times in all. 18 rows from fold line.

Place picture panel

All sts in main color continue in seed stitch as set.

Next row: Work 12 sts as set in main color, join in 1st contrast (pale pink), K48, join another ball of main color, work 12 sts as set to end.

Following row: Work 12 sts in main color, P48 in 1st contrast, work 12 sts in main color.

Repeat these 2 rows twice more. 6 rows.

Place motif

Work from adapted Elephant chart on this page. Every chart square marked with a bar symbol is in reverse stockinette: P on a right side row, K on a wrong side row.

Picture row 1: Work 12 sts in main color, K4A, place ring marker, work 40 sts from chart row 1, place ring marker, K4A, work 12 sts in main color.

Picture row 2: Work 12 sts in main color, P4A, slip marker, work 40 sts from chart row 2, slip marker, P4A, work 12 sts in main color.

Continue in this way reading from successive chart rows until chart row 52 (wrong side row) is complete. 58 picture panel rows in all. Remove markers on next row.

Next row: Work 12 sts in main color, K48 in 1st contrast (pale pink), work 12 sts in main color.

Following row: Work 12 sts in main color, P48 in 1st contrast, work 12 sts in main color.

Repeat these 2 rows twice more. 64 picture panel rows in all. Finish off 1st contrast. Finish off 2nd ball of main color. Continue in main color throughout:

Next row: Work 12 sts as set, K48, work 12 sts as set.

Change to seed stitch throughout. Work 16 rows, ending right side row.

Fold line row: K to end. 100 rows from first fold line.

Second back panel

Continue in seed stitch for a further 10 inches (25cm) ending wrong side row. Bind off in seed stitch as set.

FRINGED BORDER

With right side of work facing, using size 6 (4mm) needles and main color, pick up and K 73 sts from right side edge of Front, between the 2 fold lines.

** **Row 1 (wrong side):** K4, (K2tog, K7) 7 times, K2tog, K4. 65 sts.

Row 2: * Cast on 5 sts (using loose two-needle cast-on on page 17, Tips), bind off 4 sts, K2tog and bind off 1 st, bind off 1 more st, slip remaining st on right-hand needle back to left-hand needle, repeat from * to end, leaving last st on right-hand needle. **

Continue along loops of fold line at top of Front:
Pick up and K 72 sts. 73 sts on needle.
Repeat from ** to **.
Continue down left side edge of Front:
Pick up and K 72 sts. 73 sts on needle.
Repeat from ** to **.
Continue along loops of fold line at lower edge of Front:
Pick up and K 72 sts. 73 sts on needle.
Repeat from ** to **, binding off last st.

TO ASSEMBLE

Run in all the yarn tails and work embroidery as indicated on chart. Use pink sewing thread to sew on each sequin with a bead at its center, as described on page 55. For the tail, make a 2 inch (5cm) braid in 2nd contrast (gray), as shown on page 32, and attach as indicated on chart.

Use pearl cotton to work more flowers in single chain stitch (see page 51), scattered across the pale pink background area, following the photograph as a guide. Use pink sewing thread to sew a bead at the center of each flower.

Fold Back Panels to wrong side along fold lines, with cast-on edge overlapping bound-off edge at center back. Use main color to slip stitch side edges in place to wrong side of border rows.

TIES

On cast-on edge, mark positions for 3 ties: 1 at center, and 2 more, evenly spaced between center and each side edge.
At first position, using double-pointed needles size 6 (4mm) and main color, pick up and K 3 sts.

Work an I-cord (see page 32):
** Knit the 3 sts in the usual way. Without turning the work, push the 3 new sts along to the right end of the needle. Take the yarn tightly across the wrong side and use the other needle to knit the next row.**
Repeat from ** to ** until I-cord measures 8 inches (20cm).
Bind off.
Pull gently on the I-cord to even out the stitches.
Work 2 more I-cords at marked positions.
Work 3 more I-cords on other back panel at matching positions, spaced along a straight row of knitting, so the cords may be tied in pairs.
Insert pillow form and tie three bows on the back of the cushion.

ADAPTING DESIGNS

You can choose your own motif for any project in this book, or adapt any of our charts from the Motif Gallery to use on other suitable knitting patterns. Learn how to re-size and re-color our motifs, choose a suitable pattern and place a picture anywhere you want on your own project.

Versatile motifs

The yarn and needles you use for any project determine the gauge of your knitting, and therefore the size of any motif from our Motif Gallery.

SMALL MOTIFS

All the small motifs in the Gallery are 19 stitches wide and 26 rows deep. Check your own gauge (see page 25) for your project and then figure out the size your small motif will be:

width in inches: (19 × 4) divided by your
    number of stitches to 4 inches

width in cm: (19 × 10) divided by your
    number of stitches to 10cm

height in inches: (26 × 4) divided by your
    number of rows to 4 inches

height in cm: (26 × 10) divided by your
    number of rows to 10cm

Double knitting yarn

A typical double knitting yarn with a gauge of 22 stitches and 28 rows to 4 inches (10cm) will make a small motif measure about 3½ × 3½ inches (8.5 × 8.5cm).

Aran-weight yarn

Knitted in Aran-weight yarn, at a gauge of 18 stitches and 24 rows to 4 inches (10cm), the same motif will measure about 4¼ × 4¼ inches (10.5 × 10.5cm).

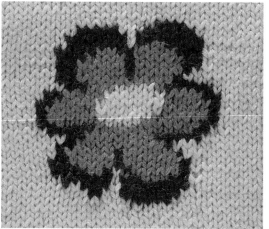

Bulky-weight yarn

Bulky-weight yarn with a gauge of 16 stitches and 20 rows to 4 inches (10cm) will make the same motif measure about 5 × 5 inches (12.5 × 12.5cm)

All the small motifs in this book are 19 stitches wide and 26 rows deep, so you can use our project instructions for the purse, scarf, hat, baby blanket, flower cushion, frog sweater or daisy sweater, and substitute any small motif(s) from the gallery to make your own individual design.

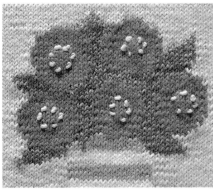

Double knitting yarn

Worked in double knitting yarn at a gauge of 22 stitches and 28 rows to 4 inches (10cm), any large motif from the Motif Gallery will measure about 7¼ x 7¼ inches (18 x 18cm).

LARGE MOTIFS

All the large motifs in the Gallery are 40 stitches wide and 52 rows deep. Again, check your own gauge to figure out the size of your chosen motif:

width in inches : (40 x 4) divided by your
 number of stitches to 4 inches

width in cm: (40 x 10) divided by your
 number of stitches to 10cm

height in inches: (52 x 4) divided by your
 number of rows to 4 inches

height in cm: (52 x 10) divided by your
 number of rows to 10cm

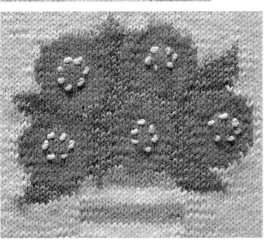

Aran-weight yarn

In Aran-weight yarn, at a gauge of 18 sts and 24 rows to 4 inches (10cm), the same motif will measure about 8¾ x 8¾ inches (22 x 22cm).

Bulky-weight yarn

Using bulky yarn, at a gauge of 16 sts and 20 rows to 4 inches (10cm), the motif will measure about 10 x 10 inches (25 x 25cm).

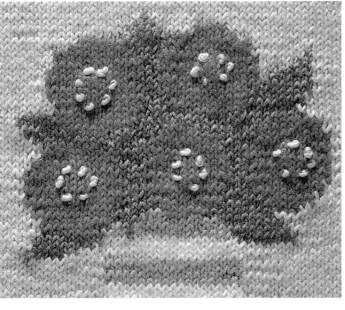

All the large motifs are 40 stitches wide and 52 rows deep, so you can adapt the instructions for the tote bag, one-panel cushion, or child's sweater by choosing any other large motif.

SUBSTITUTING COLORS

You can knit any of our motifs in your
own choice of colors. Take a little time
to check your color choice before
you begin.

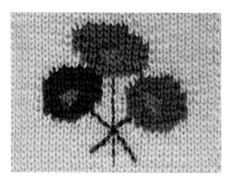

I It is a good idea to make a simple
striped swatch, with stripes of different
widths to correspond roughly with the
amount of each color used for the motif.
Pin your swatch on the wall and view it
from some distance away: is one color
too bright, or too dark? Are two colors
too close in shade? If in doubt, make
another striped swatch or two until you
find a combination you are happy with.

2 The Small Posy motif from page 102,
knitted with flowers in shades of blue
and lilac, with orange centers, on a pale
yellow background.

ADDING MOTIFS TO OTHER KNITTING PATTERNS

You can also add our motifs to other knitting instructions. The area where you place
the motif should be stockinette stitch, or another stitch of similar gauge, otherwise the
motif will be too loose or too tight, and the finished knitting will not lie flat.

I Decide where you want the motif to be. On a sweater, you might place one large
motif at the center front. One arrangement that often works well is to line up the
center of the motif with the beginning of the armhole shaping. Or you might decide to
sprinkle several smaller motifs across a sweater, on the back, front and sleeves.

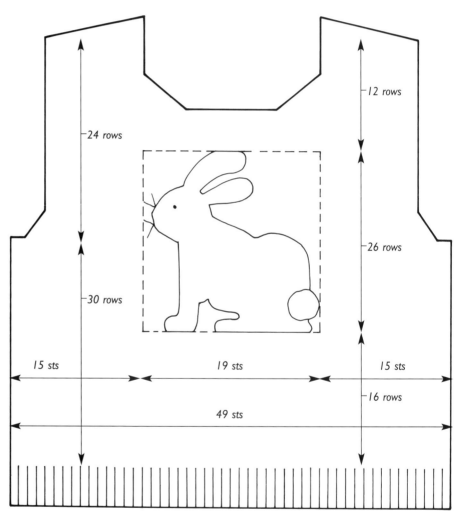

2 Draw a plan of the knitted piece (many knitting patterns these days include scale
plans of the pieces, which you could photocopy and enlarge). Write on the plan the
numbers of stitches and rows you need to make the size you want. Check your gauge
to calculate the size your motif will be (see pages 76–77). Draw a square on the plan
to represent the chart for the motif. Now you can figure out how many plain stitches
to work at each side of the charted area, and how many rows to work before you
begin the motif (make sure the motif begins on a right side row).

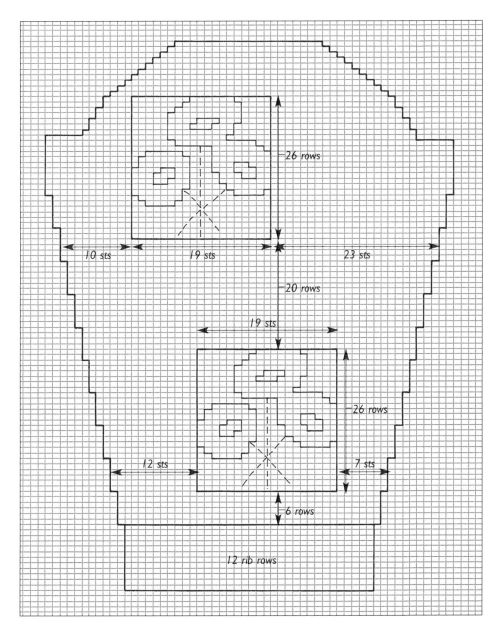

10 sts   19 sts   23 sts

26 rows

20 rows

19 sts

26 rows

12 sts   7 sts

6 rows

12 rib rows

3 For a knitted piece with complicated shaping, such as this sleeve, it is a good idea to plan the shape accurately using graph paper. A grid that corresponds to the gauge of the knitting is helpful, so photocopy our large blank grid from page 123 several times and tape the sheets together to make the size of paper you need.

Follow your pattern instructions to draw the outline of the piece, with steps for the increases and decreases. Then add a square (19 stitches × 26 rows shown here) to represent each motif, placed so that picture knitting begins on a right side row. You can now count the grid squares to knit your motif in the position you want.

PROJECT 8: Baby sweater

Knitted in a soft and cuddly Aran-weight yarn, this toddler sweater has a button shoulder and easy shaping.

SIZES

To fit approx. age: 3–6 mths, 6–12 mths, 1–2 yrs

To fit chest

18	20	22 inches
46	51	56cm

Actual measurement

21	23	25 inches
53.5	58.5	63.5cm

Length to shoulder

10	11½	13½ inches
25	29	34cm

Sleeve seam

6½	8	9¾ inches
16.5	20	25cm

Materials

Aran-weight yarn such as Debbie Bliss Cotton Angora approx.

98½ yds (90m) per 50gm:

Main color : Turquoise 200 [200, 250]gm

1st contrast : Mid-green 25gm (for all sizes)

2nd contrast: Pale green 10gm (for all sizes)

Double knitting yarn:

3rd contrast: Black scrap for embroidery

4th contrast: Orange scrap for embroidery

1 pair of needles each size 8 (5mm) (or size to obtain correct gauge) and 6 (4mm).

2 small buttons

2 ring markers

4 stitch markers

2 stitch holders (or use spare double-pointed needles)

Tapestry needle

Gauge

18 sts and 24 rows to 4 inches (10cm) measured over stockinette stitch using size 8 (5mm) needles.

Check gauge carefully as shown on page 25. Correct gauge is important for correct sizing.

Abbreviations see page 15

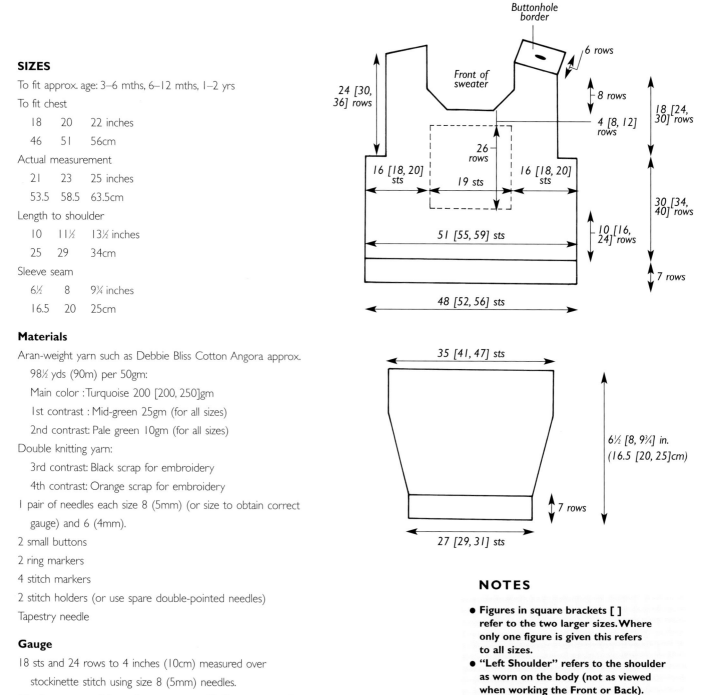

NOTES

- **Figures in square brackets [ ] refer to the two larger sizes. Where only one figure is given this refers to all sizes.**
- **"Left Shoulder" refers to the shoulder as worn on the body (not as viewed when working the Front or Back).**

Charts
- **Frog, see page 114**

BACK

Using size 6 (4mm) needles and main color (turquoise), cast on 48 [52, 56] sts. Work in garter stitch:

Row 1(wrong side row): K to end. Repeat this row, 6 more times. 7 rows. Change to size 8 (5mm) needles. Work in stockinette:

Inc row (right side row): K1, m1 tbl, K23 [25, 27], m1 tbl, K23 [25, 27], m1 tbl, K1. 51 [55, 59] sts.

Following row: K1, P to last st, K1. Work all wrong side rows of stockinette in this way *

Continue in stockinette without shaping, beginning K row, for a further 28 [32, 38] rows, ending wrong side row. 30 [34, 40] rows from last garter stitch row.

Shape armholes

Bind off 5 sts at beginning of next 2 rows. 41 [45, 49] sts.

Work without shaping for a further 22 [28, 34] rows ending wrong side row. 24 [30, 36] rows from beginning of armhole shaping.

Shape shoulders

Next row: Bind off 6 sts, K to last 6 sts, turn.

Following row: Slip 1, P to end.

Following row: Bind off 5 [6, 7] sts, K to last 11 [12, 13] sts (including the 6 sts previously unworked), turn.

Following row: P remaining 19 [21, 23] sts. Slip these 19 [21, 23] sts onto a holder. Cut yarn leaving an 8-inch (20cm) tail.

Button band

Rejoin yarn at right of remaining 11 [12, 13] sts at left shoulder. Change to size 6 (4mm) needles and garter stitch. Knit 6 rows. Bind off.

FRONT

Work as for Back to *.

Continue in stockinette, beginning K row, for a further 8 [14, 22] rows, ending wrong side row. 10 [16, 24] rows from last garter stitch row.

Place motif

Work from Frog chart on page 114, using colors as follows: A = main color (turquoise), B = 1st contrast (mid-green), C = 2nd contrast (pale green).

Next row: K16 [18, 20] A, place ring marker, K19 sts from chart row 1, place ring marker, K16 [18, 20] A.

Following row: K1A, P15 [17, 19] A, slip marker, P19 sts from chart row 2, slip marker, P15 [17, 19] A, K1A.

Continue in this way, working successive chart rows until chart row 20 [18, 16] (wrong side row) is complete. 30 [34, 40] rows from last garter stitch row.

Shape armholes

Continuing from chart in position as set, bind off 5 sts at beginning next 2 rows. 41 [45, 49] sts.

Continue without shaping until chart row 26 (wrong side row) is complete. 6 [8, 10] rows from beginning of armhole shaping.

Change to main color (turquoise) throughout. Remove markers on next row. Work a further 4 [8, 12] rows stockinette stitch, ending wrong side row. 10 [16, 22] rows from beginning of armhole shaping.

Shape front neck: first side

Next row: K15 [16, 17] sts, turn. Work on these sts only:

Following row: P2tog, P to last st, K1.

Following row: K to last 2 sts, K2tog. Repeat last 2 rows once more. 11 [12, 13] sts.

Work a further 3 stockinette rows without shaping, ending wrong side row.

Shape first shoulder and buttonhole band

Next row: K to end.

Following row: K1, P4 [5, 6], turn.

Following row: Slip 1, K to end.

Change to size 6 (4mm) needles and garter stitch. Knit 2 rows.

Buttonhole row: K4 [5, 5], bind off next 2 sts, K to end.

Following row: K, casting on 2 sts over buttonhole.

Knit a further 2 rows garter stitch ending wrong side row. Bind off.

Shape front neck: second side

With right side of work facing slip 11 [13, 15] sts at center front onto a stitch holder and rejoin main color (turquoise) at right of remaining 15 [16, 17] sts.

Next row: K to end.

Following row: K1, P to last 2 sts, P2tog tbl.

Following row: Ssk, K to end.

Repeat last 2 rows once more. 11 [12, 13] sts.

Work a further 10 stockinette rows without shaping, ending right side row.

Shape second shoulder

Next row: Bind off 6 sts (purlwise), P to last st, K1.

Following row: K to end.

Bind off remaining 5 [6, 7] sts purlwise.

SLEEVE (make 2)

Using size 6 (4mm) needles and main color (turquoise) cast on 27 [29, 31] sts. Work in garter stitch as for Back for 7 rows.

Change to size 8 (5mm) needles and stockinette:

Inc row (right side row): K1, m1 tbl, K to last st, m1 tbl, K1. 29 [31, 33] sts.

Work 5 rows stockinette, beginning and ending wrong side row. 6 rows from last garter stitch row.

Repeat the last 6 rows, 3 [5, 7] more times. 35 [41, 47] sts. 24 [36, 48] rows from last garter stitch row.

Continue without shaping until Sleeve measures 6½ [8, 9¾] inches (16.5 [20, 25]cm) from cast-on edge, ending wrong side row.

Placing a stitch marker at each end of next row, work a further 6 rows.

Bind off loosely.

NECK BORDER

Join right shoulder seam. With right side of work facing, using size 6 (4mm) needles and turquoise, pick up and K 4 sts from side edge of buttonhole border; 9 sts from first side of front neck shaping; K across 11 [13, 15] sts from holder at center front neck; pick up and K 13 sts from second side of front neck shaping; K across 19 [21, 23] sts from holder at back neck; pick up and K4 sts from side edges of button border. 60 [64, 68] sts.

Work in garter stitch for 2 rows, ending right side row.

Buttonhole row: K to last 5 sts, bind off next 2 sts, K to end.

Following row: K, casting on 2 sts over buttonhole.

Work 2 more rows garter stitch ending right side row. Bind off.

TO ASSEMBLE

Run in yarn tails on motif and work embroidery as indicated on chart. Lap buttonhole border over button border and join row ends at armhole edge. Join top edges of sleeves to armhole edges: match center of Right Sleeve to shoulder seam (and center of Left Sleeve to overlapped bands), and match rows above markers on sleeve edges to bound-off stitches of armhole shapings. Join side and sleeve seams. Sew on buttons to match buttonholes. Wash as described on page 29 or press, following instructions on ball band.

MORE IDEAS

Snake (page 114), Small Elephant (page 110), Helicopter (page 118), Small Butterfly (page 112), Two Hearts (page 94): any small motif from the Gallery will suit this baby sweater. Whatever Aran-weight yarn you choose, make sure it is soft and gentle to the touch.

PROJECT 9: Child's sweater

This child's sweater has drop shoulders and no armhole shaping, so you can concentrate on the motif. The neckband is a simple roll of stockinette. We used a fur-effect yarn for the dog, but you could choose another textured yarn, such as mohair or bouclé loop.

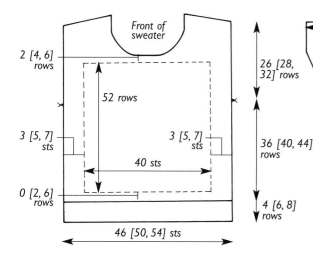

SIZES

To fit approx. age: 1–2, 3–4, 5–6 years

To fit chest

22	24	26 inches
56	61	66cm

Actual measurement

25	27½	29½ inches
63.5	70	75cm

Length to shoulder

13¾	15½	17½ inches
35	39	44cm

Sleeve seam

9¾	11½	13 inches
25	29	33cm

Materials

Bulky yarn such as Sirdar Denim Chunky
approx. 80 yds (73m) per 50gm:
Main color: Blue 250 [300, 350]gm
Equivalent fur-effect yarn, such as Sirdar Funky
Fur, used double:
1st contrast: White 50gm (for all sizes)
Equivalent bulky yarn:
2nd contrast: Pink 25gm (for all sizes)
3rd contrast: Black scrap for embroidery

1 pair needles each size 10.5 (6.5mm)
(or size to obtain correct gauge) and
9 (5.5mm)
2 ring markers
2 stitch holders or use spare double-
pointed needles
4 stitch markers

Gauge

14 sts and 19 rows to 4 inches (10cm)
measured over stockinette using size
10.5 (6.5mm) needles.
Check gauge carefully as described on
page 25. Correct gauge is crucial to
obtain the correct size.
If you are using different types of yarn for
1st and 2nd contrast colors, test their
gauge as shown on page 62.

Abbreviations see page 15

BACK

Using size 9 (5.5mm) needles and main
color (blue) cast on 46 [50, 54] sts.
Rib row 1: * K1, P1, repeat from * to
end.
Repeat this row 3 [5, 7] more times. 4
[6, 8] rib rows in all.
Change to size 10.5 (6.5mm) needles. *
Row 1: K to end.
Row 2: K1, P to last st, K1. Work all
wrong side rows of stockinette in this
way.
Repeat these 2 rows, 17 [19, 21] more
times. 36 [40, 44] rows from last rib row,
ending with a P row.
Place a marker at each end of last row,
to mark the beginning of the armhole
rows.
Repeat rows 1 and 2, 13 [14, 16] more
times. 26 [28, 32] rows in all from
markers, ending with a P row. 62 [68, 76]
rows in all from last rib row.

NOTES

- Instructions in square brackets
  [ ] refer to the two larger sizes.
  Where only one set of figures is
  given this refers to all sizes.

  Charts
- Love my dog, see page 109

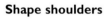

Shape shoulders

Bind off 6 [7, 7] sts at beginning next 2 rows, knitwise on K row, purlwise on P row.

Bind off 7 [7, 8] sts at beginning following 2 rows. 20 [22, 24] sts remain.

Slip these sts onto a stitch holder and cut yarn leaving a 12-inch (30-cm) tail for assembly.

FRONT

Work as given for Back to *.

Work in stockinette as given for Back for 0 [2, 6] rows, ending with a wrong side row. (Note: for first size only, motif begins immediately after rib rows.)

Place motif

Work from Love My Dog chart (page 109), using colors as follows: A = main color (blue); B = 1st contrast (white); C = 2nd contrast (pink).

Chart row 1: K3 [5, 7] A, place ring marker, K40 sts from chart row 1, place ring marker, K3 [5, 7] A.

Chart row 2: K1 A, P2 [4, 6] A, slip marker, P40 sts from chart row 2, P2 [4, 6] A, K1 A.

Continue in this way, reading from successive chart rows and placing a stitch marker at each end of chart row 36 [38, 38].

Continue until chart row 52 is complete.

Continue in main color (blue) for a further 2 [4, 6] rows, thus ending P row.

Shape front neck: first side

Next row: K18 [20, 21] sts, turn. Work on these sts only:

Following row: P2tog, P to last st, K1.

Following row: K to last 2 sts, K2tog.

Repeat 2nd and 3rd neck rows 1 [2, 2] more times.

First size only

Work 2nd neck row once again.

All sizes

13 [14, 15] sts remain. Work 2 [3, 5] more rows, ending P row. 62 [68, 76]

rows in all from last rib row, matching Back at beginning of shoulder shaping.

Shape shoulder

Next row: Bind off 6 [7, 7] sts knitwise, K to end.

Following row: P to end.
Bind off remaining 7 [7, 8] sts knitwise.
Cut yarn leaving a 12-inch (30cm) tail for assembly.

Shape front neck: second side

With right side of Front facing, slip 10 [10, 12] sts at center onto a stitch holder and rejoin main color (blue) at right of remaining 18 [20, 21] sts.

Next row: K to end.

Following row: P to last 2 sts, P2tog tbl.

Following row: Ssk, K to end.
Repeat 2nd and 3rd neck rows, 1 [2, 2] more times.

1st size only

Work 2nd neck row once again.

All sizes

13 [14, 15] sts remain. Work 3 [4, 6] more rows, ending K row.

Shape shoulder

Next row: Bind off 6 [7, 7] sts

purlwise, P to end.

Following row: K to end.
Bind off remaining 7 [7, 8] sts purlwise.
Cut yarn leaving a 12-inch (30-cm) tail for assembly.

SLEEVE (make 2)

Using size 9 (5.5mm) needles and main color (blue) cast on 28 [28, 30] sts.

Rib row 1: * K1, P1, repeat from * to end.
Repeat this row 5 more times. 6 rib rows in all.
Change to size 10.5 (6.5mm) needles.

Shape sleeve

Inc row 1: K1, m1 tbl, K to last st, m1 tbl, K1. 30 [30, 32] sts.
Work 5 rows stockinette, beginning and ending P row.
Repeat these 6 rows, 4 [6, 7] more times. 38 [42, 46] sts. 30 [42, 48] rows in all from last rib row.
Continue in stockinette for a further 12 [8, 8] rows ending P row. 42 [50, 56] rows in all from last rib row. Bind off loosely.

NECKBAND

Join left shoulder seam with backstitch using end left for this purpose. With right

side of work facing, using size 9 (5.5mm) needles and main color (blue), K across 20 [22, 24] sts from holder at back neck; pick up and K10 [11, 11] sts from first side of front neck shaping; K across 10 [10, 12] sts from holder at center front; pick up and K10 [11, 11] sts from second side of front neck shaping. 50 [54, 58] sts.
Beginning with a P row, work 9 rows stockinette, ending P row.
Change to a size 10.5 (6.5mm) needle and bind off loosely.

TO ASSEMBLE

Run in all yarn ends from motif. Work embroidery using 3rd contrast, as shown on chart.
Join remaining shoulder and neckband seam. Allow the neckband to form a roll. Fold one Sleeve in half lengthwise to find center of top edge. Match this point to shoulder seam. Match top corners of Sleeve to markers on side edges of Back and Front. Using mattress stitch (see page 28), join armhole seam. Join top edge of other Sleeve to armhole in same way. Join side and sleeve seams using mattress stitch, taking selvage stitches into seams. Run in any remaining yarn ends along seams. Wash as described on page 29 or press, following instructions on ball bands.

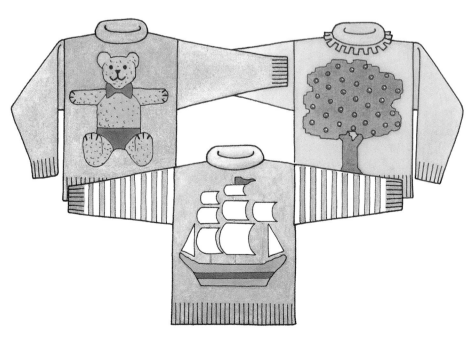

MORE IDEAS

Any large motif from the Gallery will suit this child's sweater. You could choose the Large Ted (page 117), and use a furry yarn for his body; or knit the Pirate Ship (page 119), adding white stripes to the sleeves; or choose the Tree (page 107), and add a Fringed Border (as Project 7, page 70) to the neckband.

PROJECT 10: Teen sweater

Neat set-in sleeves and a pretty looped border show off your knitting skills on this pretty sweater. The daisy motifs are worked in three colors and decorated with embroidery and mother-of-pearl buttons.

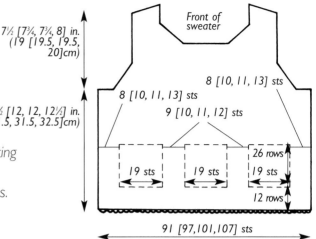

7½ [7¾, 7¾, 8] in. (19 [19.5, 19.5, 20]cm)

11½ [12, 12, 12½] in. (30 [31.5, 31.5, 32.5]cm)

Front of sweater

8 [10, 11, 13] sts

8 [10, 11, 13] sts

9 [10, 11, 12] sts

26 rows

19 sts   19 sts   19 sts

12 rows

91 [97,101,107] sts

SIZE

To fit bust

32	34	36	38 inches
81	86	91	96cm

Actual measurement

36	38	40	42 inches
91	96	101	106cm

Length to shoulder

19	19¾	19¾	20½ inches
49	51	51	52.5 cm

Sleeve seam

17	17½	18	18½ inches
43	44.5	46	47cm

Materials

Double Knitting Cotton such as Rowan Handknit DK Cotton approx. 93 yds (85m) per 50gm:

Main color: Ecru 450 [450, 500, 550]gm

1st contrast: Ice blue 50gm (for all sizes)

2nd contrast: Sugar pink 50gm (for all sizes)

3rd contrast: Lilac 50gm (for all sizes)

1 pair of needles each size 6 (4mm) (or size to obtain correct gauge) and 5 (3.5mm)

6 ring markers

2 stitch holders

Tapestry needle

8 mother-of-pearl buttons, optional

Anti-fray solution

Gauge

20 sts and 28 rows to 4 inches (10cm) measured over stockinette using size 6 (4mm) needles.

Check gauge carefully as described on page 25.

Correct gauge is crucial to obtain the correct size.

Abbreviations see page 15

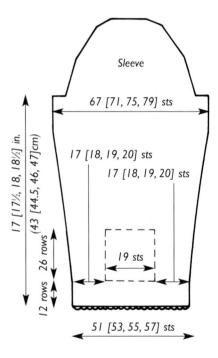

Sleeve

67 [71, 75, 79] sts

17 [18, 19, 20] sts

17 [18, 19, 20] sts

17 [17½, 18, 18½] in. (43 [44.5, 46, 47]cm)

26 rows

12 rows

19 sts

51 [53, 55, 57] sts

NOTES

- **Figures in square brackets [ ] refer to the three larger sizes. Where only one figure is given this refers to all sizes.**
- **Lower borders and cuffs are knitted downward after pieces are complete.**

Charts
- **Daisy, see page 102**

BACK

Using size 6 (4mm) needles and main color (ecru), cast on 91 [97, 101, 107] sts. Work in stockinette:

Row 1: K to end.

Row 2: K1, P to last st, K1. Work all wrong side rows of stockinette in this way. Repeat these 2 rows, 5 more times. 12 rows.

Place motifs

Each Daisy motif is worked in a different color (from right to left: blue, pink, lilac). Follow the Daisy chart on page 102, using colors as follows: A = main color (ecru), B = 1st contrast (blue), 2nd contrast (pink) or 3rd contrast (lilac), C = main color (ecru).

Row 13: K8 [10, 11, 13] A, place ring marker, K19 sts from chart row 1 using 1st contrast (blue) for B, place ring marker, K9 [10, 11, 12] A, place ring marker, K19 sts from chart row 1 using

2nd contrast (pink) for B, place ring marker, K9 [10, 11, 12] A, place ring marker, K19 sts from chart row 1 using 3rd contrast (lilac) for B, place ring marker, K8 [10, 11, 13]A.

Row 14: K1A, P7 [9, 10, 12] A, * slip marker, P19 sts from chart row 2, slip marker, P9 [10, 11, 12] A, * repeat from * to * once more, slip marker, P19 sts from chart row 2, slip marker, P7 [9, 10, 12] A, K1A.

Continue in this way, working successive chart rows until chart row 26 (wrong side row) is complete. 38 rows in all. Change to main color (ecru). Removing markers on next row, repeat rows 1 and 2 until work measures 11 [11½, 11½, 12] inches (28 [29, 29, 30]cm) in all ending wrong side row.

Shape armholes

Continue in stockinette throughout. Bind off 6 sts at beginning next 2 rows. 79 [85, 89, 95] sts.

Dec row 1: K1, ssk, K to last 3 sts, K2tog, K1.

Dec row 2: K1, P to last st, K1. Repeat these 2 rows, 6 [7, 7, 8] more times. 65 [69, 73, 77] sts remain. **
Continue without shaping until work measures 18½ [19¼, 19¼, 20] inches (47 [49, 49, 51]cm) in all ending wrong side row.

Shape shoulders

Bind off 7 [8, 8, 9] sts at beginning next 2 rows.
Bind off 8 [8, 9, 9] sts at beginning following 2 rows.
Slip remaining 35 [37, 39, 41] sts onto a stitch holder.

Lower border

With right side of work facing, using size 5 (3.5mm) needles and main color (ecru), pick up and K1 st from each st along cast-on edge, working twice into last st. 91 [97, 101, 107] sts.
*** K2 rows.

Looped bind-off row (wrong side row):

K1, * K1, (yarn around needle, lift previous stitch over) 9 times, forming a 9-chain loop; on right-hand needle, lift previous stitch over 9th chain; bind off next stitch in the usual way *, repeat from * to * to end.

FRONT

Work as given for Back to **, but with the flower motifs in colors as follows (right to left): 2nd contrast (pink), 1st contrast (blue), 3rd contrast (lilac). Continue without shaping until work measures 15½ [16, 16, 16½] inches (39.5 [40.5, 40.5, 42]cm) in all ending wrong side row.

Shape neck: first side

Next row: K26 [27, 28, 29], turn. Work on these sts only.
Following row: P2tog tbl, P to last st, K1.
Following row: K to last 2 sts, ssk. Repeat last 2 rows twice more, and wrong side row once again. 19 [20, 21, 22] sts.
Next row: K to last 2 sts, K2tog.
Following row: P to last st, K1. Repeat these 2 rows, 3 more times. 15 [16, 17, 18] sts.
Continue without shaping until Front length matches Back at beginning of shoulder shaping, ending wrong side row.

Shape shoulder

Bind off 7 [8, 8, 9] sts at beginning next

row, work to end.
Work 1 wrong side row. Bind off remaining 8 [8, 9, 9] sts.

Front neck: second side

With right side of work facing, slip 13 [15, 17, 19] sts at center front onto a stitch holder.
Rejoin main color at right of remaining 26 [27, 28, 29] sts and K to end.
Next row: K1, P to last 2 sts, P2tog.
Following row: K2tog, K to end. Repeat these 2 rows twice more and wrong side row once again. 19 [20, 21, 22] sts.
Next row: K2tog, K to end.
Following row: K1, P to end. Repeat these 2 rows, 3 more times. 15 [16, 17, 18] sts.
Continue without shaping until length matches Back at beginning of shoulder shaping, ending right side row.

Shape shoulder

Bind off 7 [8, 8, 9] sts purlwise at beginning next row, P to last st, K1. Work 1 right side row. Bind off remaining 8 [8, 9, 9] sts purlwise.

Lower border

Work to match Back Lower Border.

LEFT SLEEVE

Using size 6 (4mm) needles and main color (ecru) cast on 51 [53, 55, 57] sts. Work in stockinette as for Back for 10 rows, ending wrong side row.
Inc row: K1, m1 tbl, K to last st, m1 tbl, K1.
Work 1 wrong side row. 53 [55, 57, 59] sts. 12 rows in all.

Place motif

Row 13: K17 [18, 19, 20] A, place ring marker, K19 sts from chart row 1 using 1st contrast (blue) for B and main color (ecru) for A and C, place ring marker, K17 [18, 19, 20] A.

Row 14: K1A, P16 [17, 18, 19] A, slip marker, P19 sts from chart row 2, slip marker, P16 [17, 18, 19] A, K1A.

Continue in this way reading from successive chart rows and inc 1 st at each end chart rows 9 and 19, until chart row 26 (wrong side row) is complete. 57 [59, 61, 63] sts. 38 rows in all.

Continue in main color and stockinette, inc 1 st at each end 3rd and every following 10th row until there are 67 [71, 75, 79] sts.

Continue without shaping until Sleeve measures 16½ [17, 17.5, 18] inches (42 [43, 44.5, 46]cm) in all (or length required), ending wrong side row.

Shape sleeve head

Bind off 6 sts at beginning next 2 rows.

Dec row 1: K1, ssk, K to last 3 sts, K2tog, K1.

Dec row 2: K1, P to last st, K1.

Dec row 3: K to end.

Dec row 4: K1, P to last st, K1.

Repeat these 4 rows twice more. 49 [53, 57, 61] sts remain.

Repeat dec rows 1 and 2, 7 [8, 10, 11] times in all. 35 [37, 37, 39] sts remain.

Bind off 4 sts at beginning next 4 rows.

Bind off remaining 19 [21, 21, 23] sts.

Lower border

With right side of work facing, using size 5 (3.5mm) needles and main color, pick up and K 1 st from each st along cast-on edge, working twice into last st. 51 [53, 55, 57] sts.

Complete as Back Lower Border from *** to end.

RIGHT SLEEVE

Work to match Left Sleeve, using 2nd contrast (pink) for B on the Daisy motif.

NECK BORDER

Join left shoulder seam. With right side of work facing, using size 5 (3.5mm) needles and main color (ecru), K across 35 [37, 39, 41] sts from holder at back neck; pick up and K 18 [19, 20, 21] sts from first side of front neck shaping; K across 13 [15, 17, 19] sts from holder at front neck; pick up and K 19 [20, 21, 22] sts from second side of front neck shaping. 85 [91, 97, 103] sts.

Complete as Back Lower Border from *** to end.

TO ASSEMBLE

Run in yarn tails on motifs. Before finishing, add embroidery if you wish.

Optional embroidery

Use tapestry needle to embroider 5 single chain stitches (see page 51) on each daisy, using colors as follows: 2nd contrast (pink) on daisies in 1st contrast (blue); 3rd contrast (lilac) on daisies in 2nd contrast (pink); 1st contrast (blue) on daisies in 3rd contrast (lilac). Begin by leaving a 4-inch (10cm) tail (as on page 51). Before fastening off the embroidery yarn, bring needle through to right side at

center of daisy and use same yarn to sew on a mother-of-pearl button with a single stitch. Make a small backstitch behind the button, and then tie the two ends very firmly with a reef knot behind the button. Trim the tails to ¼ inch (6mm). Paint the knot with anti-fray solution (Thread Magic or Fraycheck) and leave to dry.

Join remaining shoulder seam and neck border seam. Join sleeve heads to armhole edges, matching center of each sleeve head to shoulder seam. Join side and sleeve seams. Wash as shown on page 29 or press, according to instructions on ball band.

MORE IDEAS

Choose any small motif from the Gallery for this sweater, such as the Double Heart (page 94) or Strawberries (page 106). You can vary the colors of the motifs as for the Daisies above, or choose to knit them all in the same color combination. You can add your own choice of embroidery, beads, or sequins. You could even choose several different motifs, like the Pansy (page 99), Lily (page 99), and Small Rose (page 101), and use them all on one sweater!

MOTIF GALLERY

Hearts, stars, flowers, fruit, animals, toys. Take your pick! Follow our suggested colors, or substitute colors of your choice. Learn how to add a name or slogan, and how to draw a chart for a design of your own.

Small heart

A Cream
    Join in
    Finish off

B Dark pink
△ Join in
▽ Finish off

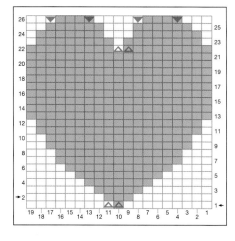

Use on: Purse, hat, four-panel cushion

Double heart

A Pale pink
△ Join in
▽ Finish off

B Dark pink
△ Join in
▽ Finish off

C Peach
△ Join in
▽ Finish off

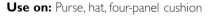

Use on: Baby blanket, baby sweater, teen sweater

Two hearts

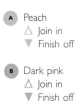

A Peach
△ Join in
▽ Finish off

B Dark pink
△ Join in
▽ Finish off

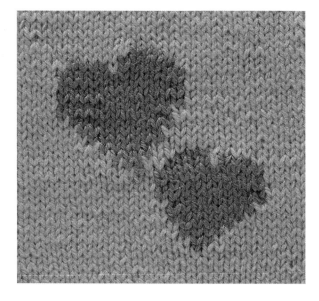

Use on: Purse, four-panel cushion, baby sweater

Large heart

A Cream
    Join in
    Finish off

B Dark pink
  △ Join in
  ▽ Finish off
  ● French knot

C Peach
  △ Join in
  ▽ Finish off

D Pale pink
  △ Join in
  ▽ Finish off

E Lilac
  △ Join in
  ▽ Finish off

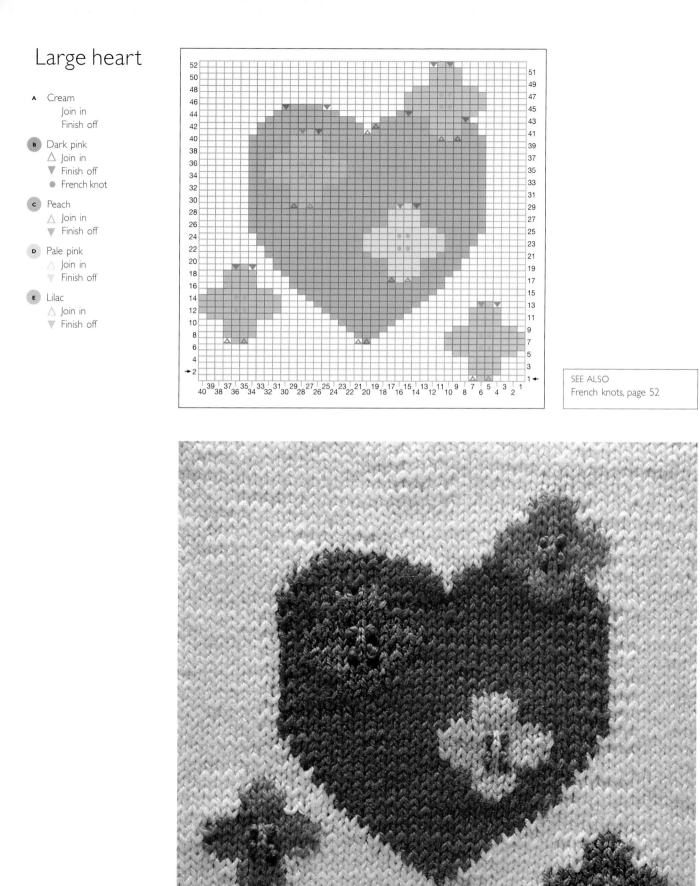

SEE ALSO
French knots, page 52

Use on: Tote bag,
one-panel cushion,
child's sweater

Small sun

A Pale blue
     Join in
     ∨ Finish off

B Orange
     △ Join in
     ▼ Finish off
     ∨ Duplicate stitch

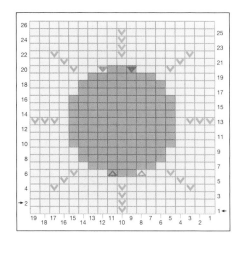

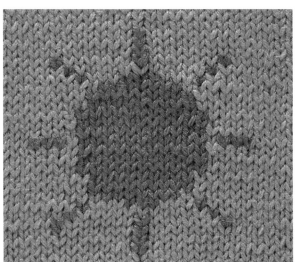

Use on: Scarf, hat, baby sweater

Moon

A Dark blue
     △ Join in
     ▼ Finish off
     ∨ Duplicate stitch

B Cream
     △ Join in
     ▽ Finish off

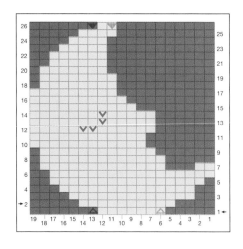

Use on: Baby blanket, baby sweater

Small star

A Dark blue
     △ Join in
     ▼ Finish off

B Yellow
     △ Join in
     ▽ Finish off

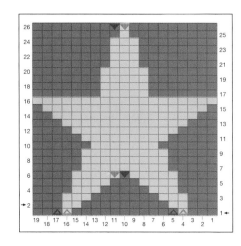

Use on: Scarf, hat, baby blanket

Large sun

A Pale blue
     Join in
    ▽ Finish off

B Orange
    △ Join in
    ▼ Finish off
    ∨ Duplicate stitch

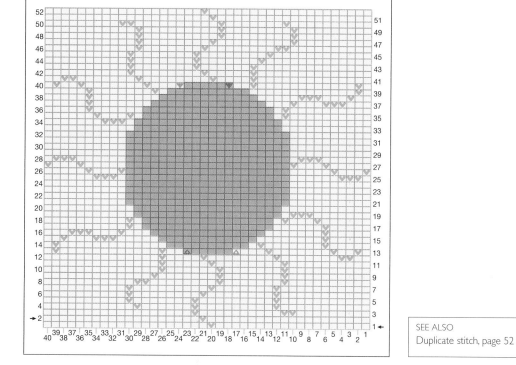

SEE ALSO
Duplicate stitch, page 52

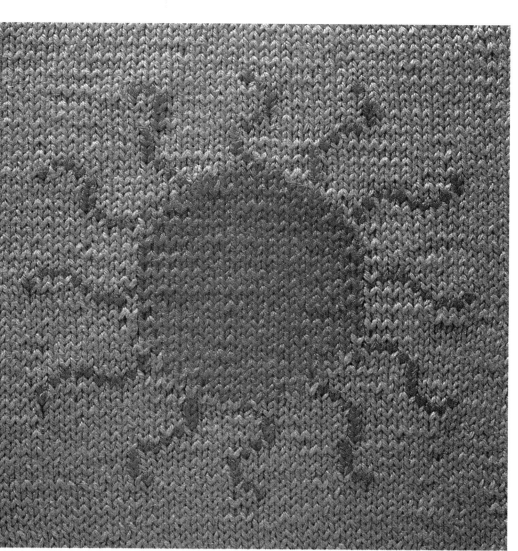

Use on: Tote bag, child's
           sweater

Large stars

A Dark blue
△ Join in
▼ Finish off

B Yellow
△ Join in
▼ Finish off

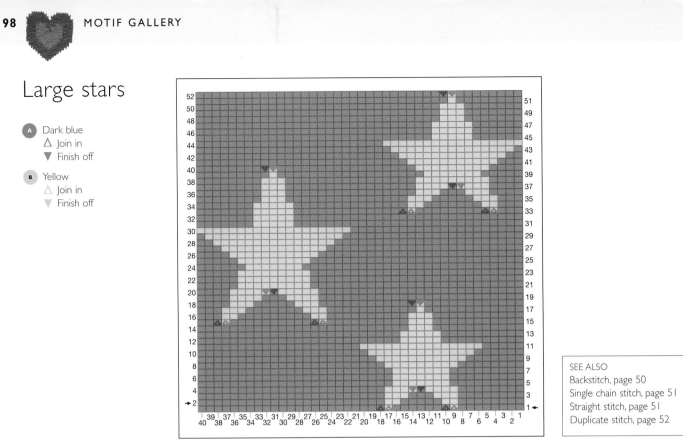

SEE ALSO
Backstitch, page 50
Single chain stitch, page 51
Straight stitch, page 51
Duplicate stitch, page 52

Use on: Tote bag, child's sweater

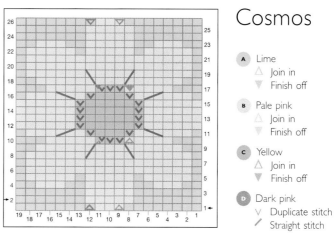

Cosmos

A Lime
  △ Join in
  ▽ Finish off

B Pale pink
  △ Join in
  ▽ Finish off

C Yellow
  △ Join in
  ▽ Finish off

D Dark pink
  V Duplicate stitch
  ╱ Straight stitch

Use on: Purse, four-panel cushion

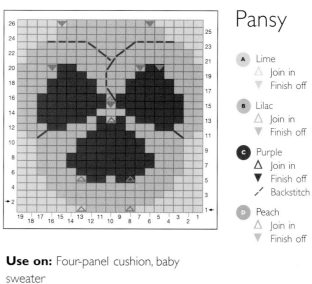

Pansy

A Lime
  △ Join in
  ▽ Finish off

B Lilac
  △ Join in
  ▽ Finish off

C Purple
  △ Join in
  ▼ Finish off
  ╱ Backstitch

D Peach
  △ Join in
  ▽ Finish off

Use on: Four-panel cushion, baby sweater

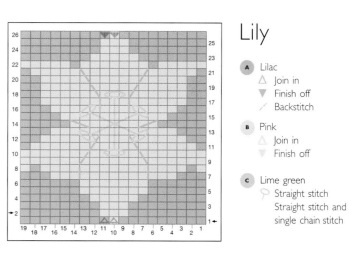

Lily

A Lilac
  △ Join in
  ▽ Finish off
  ╱ Backstitch

B Pink
  △ Join in
  ▽ Finish off

C Lime green
  ♀ Straight stitch
  Straight stitch and
  single chain stitch

Use on: Purse, four-panel cushion

Large roses

A Lime
△ Join in
▽ Finish off

B Pale-pink
△ Join in
▽ Finish off

C Mid-pink
∨ Duplicate stitch

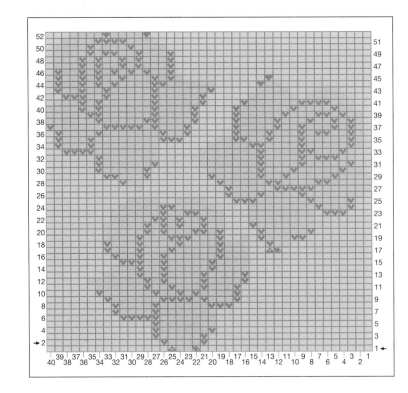

SEE ALSO
Duplicate stitch, page 52

Use on: Tote bag, one-panel cushion

Small rose

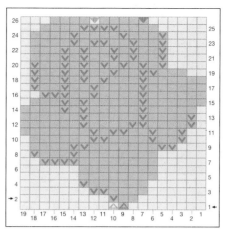

A Pale pink
△ Join in
▽ Finish off

B Mid-pink
△ Join in
▽ Finish off

C Dark pink
∨ Duplicate stitch

Use on: Purse, four-panel cushion

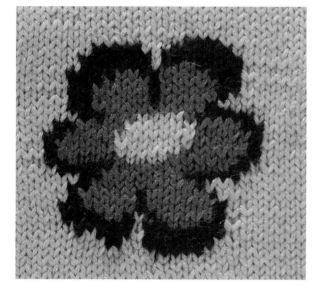

Peony

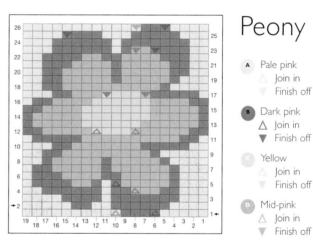

A Pale pink
△ Join in
▽ Finish off

B Dark pink
△ Join in
▼ Finish off

C Yellow
△ Join in
▽ Finish off

D Mid-pink
△ Join in
▽ Finish off

Use on: Scarf, hat, four-panel cushion

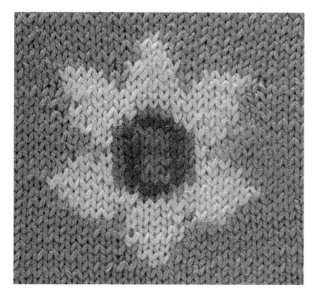

Daffodil

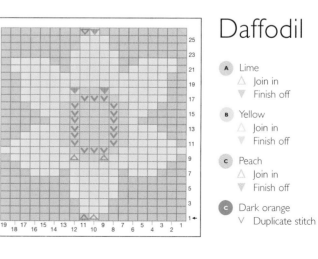

A Lime
△ Join in
▽ Finish off

B Yellow
△ Join in
▽ Finish off

C Peach
△ Join in
▽ Finish off

C Dark orange
∨ Duplicate stitch

Use on: Scarf, hat, four-panel cushion

Small daisy

A Turquoise
△ Join in
▽ Finish off

B Dark pink
△ Join in
▼ Finish off

C Lilac
△ Join in
▽ Finish off

D Orange
△ Join in
▼ Finish off

E Yellow
Join in
Finish off

F Green
╱ Backstitch

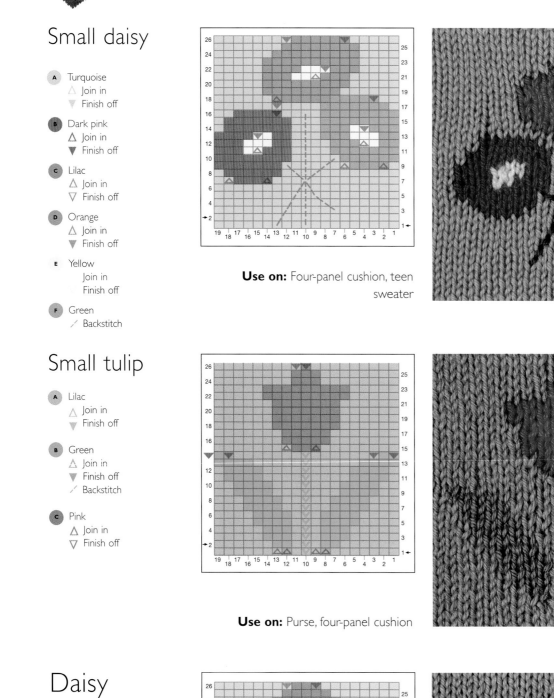

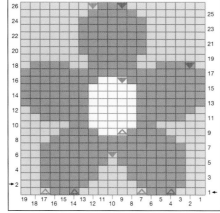

Use on: Four-panel cushion, teen sweater

Small tulip

A Lilac
△ Join in
▼ Finish off

B Green
△ Join in
▼ Finish off
╱ Backstitch

C Pink
△ Join in
▽ Finish off

Use on: Purse, four-panel cushion

Daisy

A Aqua
△ Join in
▽ Finish off

B Lilac
△ Join in
▼ Finish off

C Yellow
Join in
Finish off

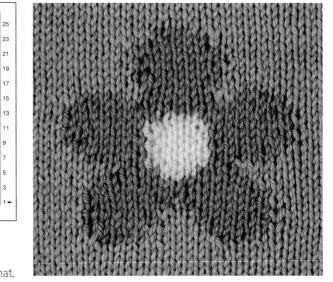

Use on: Purse, scarf, hat, teen sweater

Large tulips

A Lilac
△ Join in
▽ Finish off

B Green
△ Join in
▽ Finish off
╱ Backstitch

C Dark pink
△ Join in
▽ Finish off

D Orange
△ Join in
▽ Finish off

E Light red
△ Join in
▽ Finish off

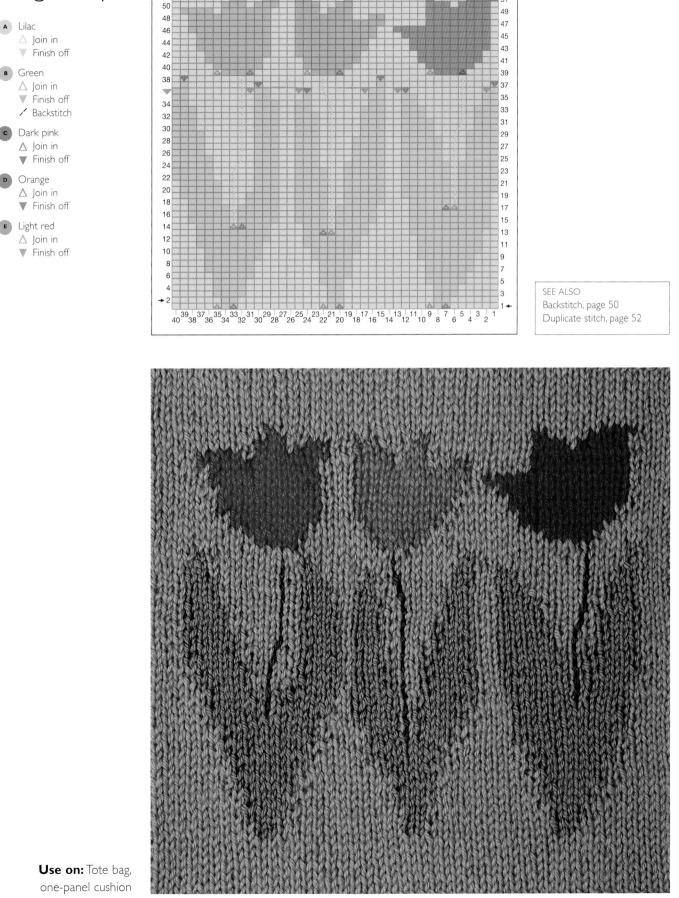

SEE ALSO
Backstitch, page 50
Duplicate stitch, page 52

Use on: Tote bag,
one-panel cushion

Flowerpot

A Yellow
  Join in
  Finish off
  French knot

B Aqua blue
  △ Join in
  ▼ Finish off

C White
  △ Join in
  ▼ Finish off

D Green
  △ Join in
  ▼ Finish off

E Mid-pink
  △ Join in
  ▼ Finish off

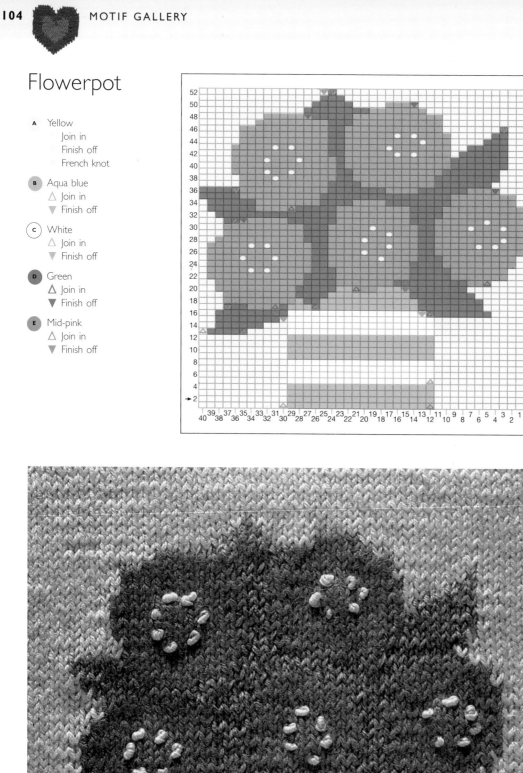

Use on: Tote bag, one-panel cushion

Large posy

A Aqua blue
△ Join in
▽ Finish off

B Orange
△ Join in
▽ Finish off

C Mid-pink
△ Join in
▽ Finish off

D Yellow
Join in
Finish off

E Green
╱ Back stitch
○ Single chain stitch
✕ Sew on bow made from
8 inches (20cm) braid,
or ribbon

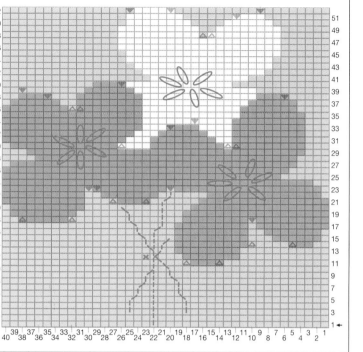

SEE ALSO
Braids, page 32
Backstitch, page 50
Single chain stitch, page 51
French knots, page 52

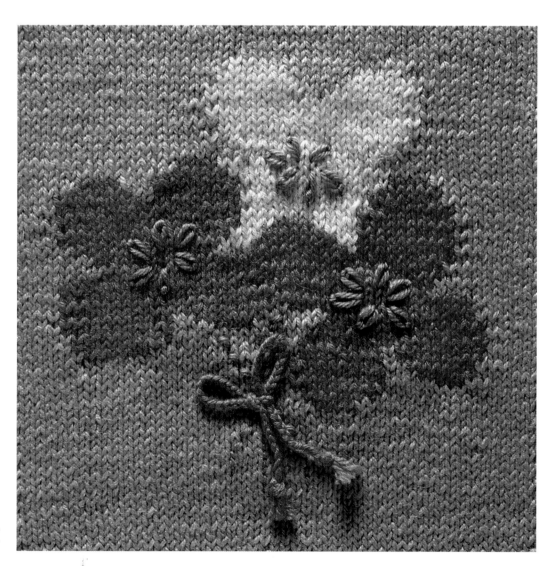

Use on: Tote bag,
child's sweater

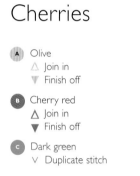

Apple

A Yellow
  Join in
  Finish off

B Apple green
  △ Join in
  ▽ Finish off

C Dark pink
  △ Join in
  ▽ Finish off

D Dark green
  △ Join in
  ▽ Finish off

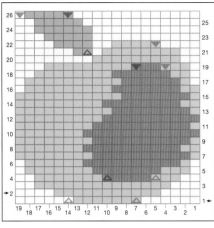

Use on: Purse, baby sweater

Cherries

A Olive
  △ Join in
  ▽ Finish off

B Cherry red
  △ Join in
  ▽ Finish off

C Dark green
  ∨ Duplicate stitch

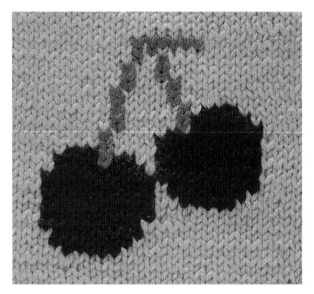

Use on: Baby sweater, teen sweater

Strawberries

A Yellow
  Join in
  Finish off
  Duplicate stitch

B Red
  △ Join in
  ▽ Finish off

C Dark pink
  △ Join in
  ▽ Finish off

D Green
  ∨ Duplicate stitch

Use on: Purse, baby sweater,
teen sweater

Tree

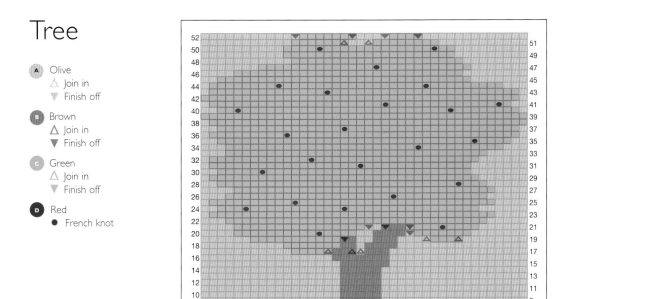

- **A** Olive
  - △ Join in
  - ▽ Finish off
- **B** Brown
  - △ Join in
  - ▽ Finish off
- **C** Green
  - △ Join in
  - ▽ Finish off
- **D** Red
  - ● French knot

SEE ALSO
Duplicate stitch, page 52
French knots, page 52

Use on: Tote bag,
child's sweater

Small dog

- **A** Pale blue
  - △ Join in
  - ▽ Finish off
- **B** Brown
  - △ Join in
  - ▽ Finish off
- **C** Black
  - ● French knot
  - V Duplicate stitch
  - ╱ Straight stitch

Use on: Baby blanket, baby sweater

Cat

- **A** Pale blue
  - △ Join in
  - ▽ Finish off
- **B** Orange
  - △ Join in
  - ▽ Finish off
- **C** Black
  - ● French knot
  - ╱ Straight stitch

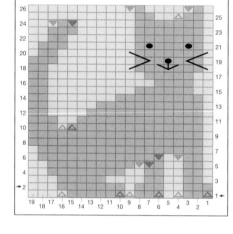

Use on: Purse, baby blanket

Rabbit

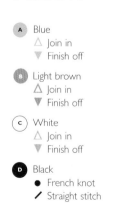

- **A** Blue
  - △ Join in
  - ▽ Finish off
- **B** Light brown
  - △ Join in
  - ▽ Finish off
- **C** White
  - △ Join in
  - ▽ Finish off
- **D** Black
  - ● French knot
  - ╱ Straight stitch

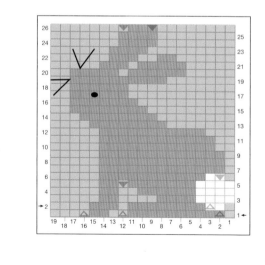

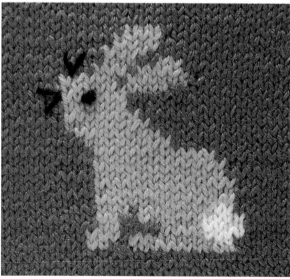

Use on: Baby blanket, baby sweater

Love my dog

A Blue
△ Join in
▽ Finish off
  Backstitch

B Brown
△ Join in
▽ Finish off

C Dark pink
△ Join in
▽ Finish off

D Black
∨ Duplicate stitch

TIP

**Sometimes
embroidered eyes
and whiskers look
better if you work
them in a finer yarn.
For example, if you
are knitting in Aran-
weight yarn, try
double knitting for
the embroidered
details.**

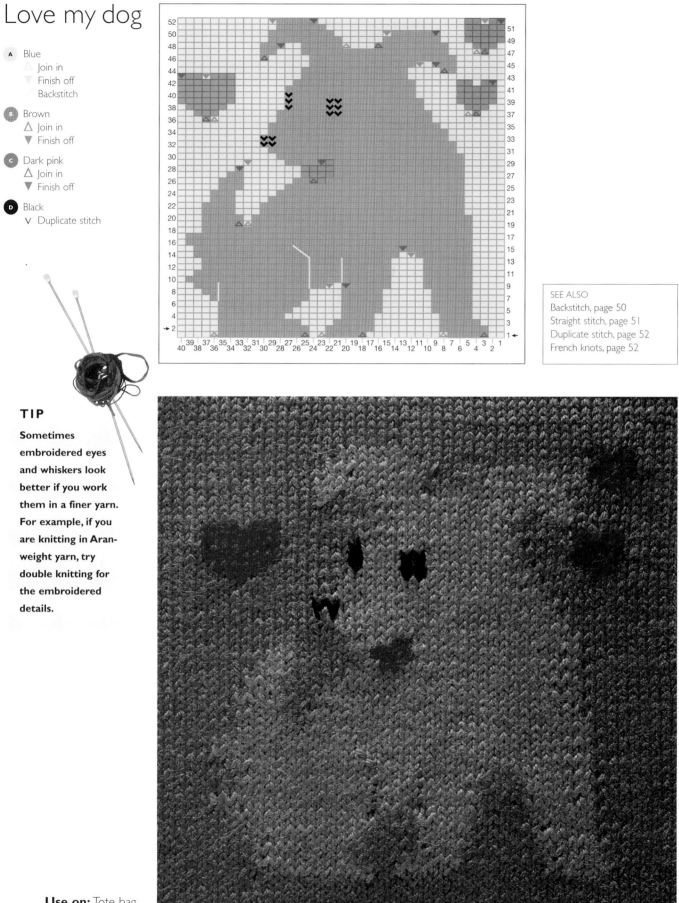

SEE ALSO
Backstitch, page 50
Straight stitch, page 51
Duplicate stitch, page 52
French knots, page 52

Use on: Tote bag,
child's sweater

Duck

A Turquoise
△ Join in
▽ Finish off

B White
△ Join in
▽ Finish off

C Orange
△ Join in
▽ Finish off
╱ Backstitch

D Black
● French knot

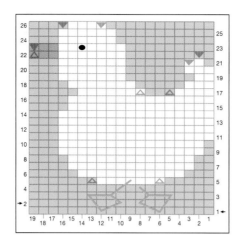

Use on: Baby blanket, baby sweater

Small elephant

A Pink
△ Join in
▽ Finish off
╱ Backstitch

B Gray
△ Join in
▽ Finish off
✕ Sew on braid tail
1¼ inches (3cm) long

C Black
● French knot

D White
═ Single chain stitch

Use on: Baby blanket, baby sweater

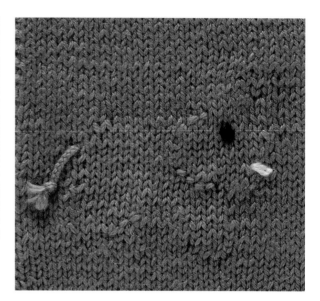

Mouse

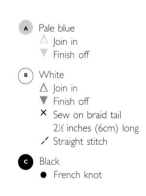

A Pale blue
△ Join in
▽ Finish off

B White
△ Join in
▽ Finish off
✕ Sew on braid tail
2½ inches (6cm) long
╱ Straight stitch

C Black
● French knot

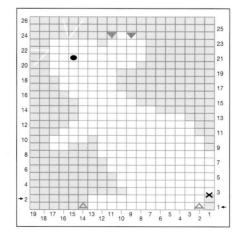

Use on: Baby blanket, baby sweater

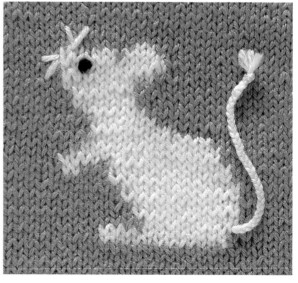

Large elephant

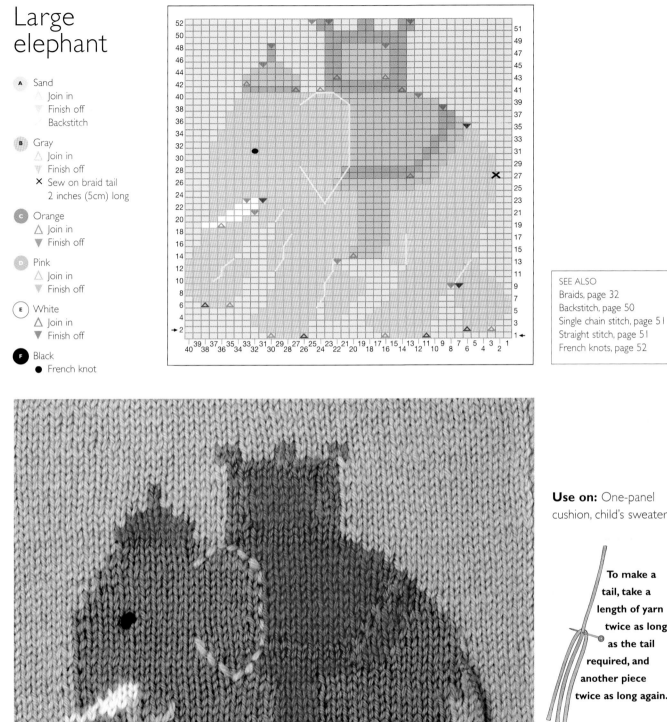

A Sand
△ Join in
▽ Finish off
Backstitch

B Gray
△ Join in
▽ Finish off
✕ Sew on braid tail
2 inches (5cm) long

C Orange
△ Join in
▽ Finish off

D Pink
△ Join in
▽ Finish off

E White
△ Join in
▽ Finish off

F Black
● French knot

SEE ALSO
Braids, page 32
Backstitch, page 50
Single chain stitch, page 51
Straight stitch, page 51
French knots, page 52

Use on: One-panel cushion, child's sweater

To make a tail, take a length of yarn twice as long as the tail required, and another piece twice as long again.

Tie an overhand knot at the end and trim the ends to form a little tassel. Use the single length at the top to sew the tail in place.

Small butterfly

(A) White
△ Join in
▼ Finish off

(B) Pink
△ Join in
▼ Finish off

(C) Blue
∨ Duplicate stitch

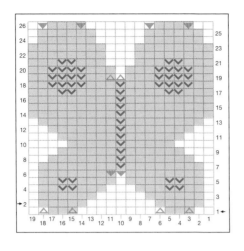

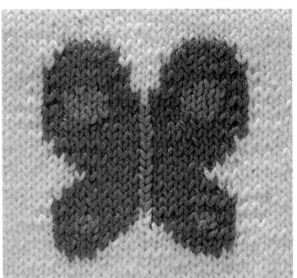

Use on: Baby blanket, baby sweater

Bird

(A) White
△ Join in
▼ Finish off

(B) Blue
△ Join in
▼ Finish off

(C) Black
● French knot
╱ Straight stitch

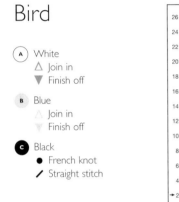

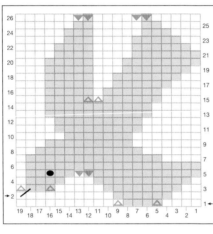

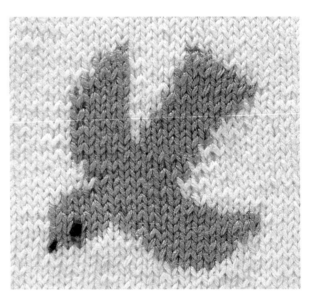

Use on: Hat, baby blanket

Bee

(A) Pale blue
△ Join in
▼ Finish off
╱ Backstitch

(B) Black
△ Join in
▼ Finish off
╱ Backstitch

(C) Yellow
△ Join in
▼ Finish off

(D) White
△ Join in
▼ Finish off

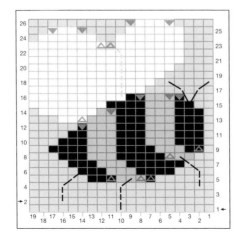

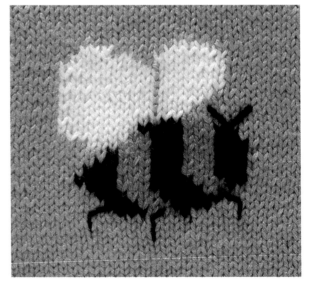

Use on: Four-panel cushion, baby blanket

Large butterfly

A Pink
  △ Join in
  ▽ Finish off

B White
  △ Join in
  ▼ Finish off

C Pale blue
  △ Join in
  ▽ Finish off
  ⟋ Backstitch
  ● French knot

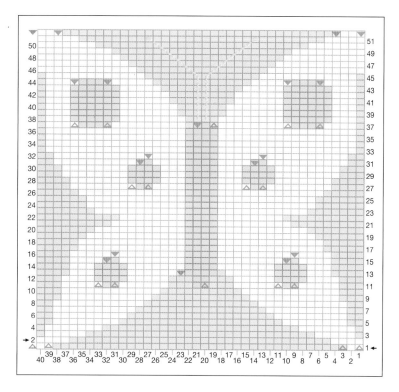

SEE ALSO
Backstitch, page 50
Straight stitch, page 51
Duplicate stitch, page 52
French knots, page 52

Use on: Tote bag, one-panel cushion

Small fish

A Turquoise
△ Join in
▽ Finish off

B Orange
△ Join in
▽ Finish off

C Black
● French knot

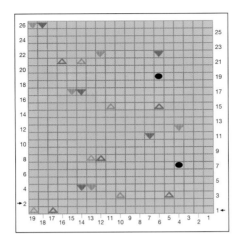

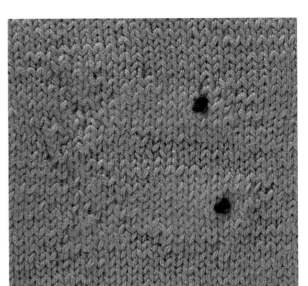

Use on: Scarf, hat, baby sweater

Snake

A Sand
△ Join in
▽ Finish off

B Green
△ Join in
▽ Finish off

C Black
● French knot
/ Backstitch

D Orange
/ Backstitch

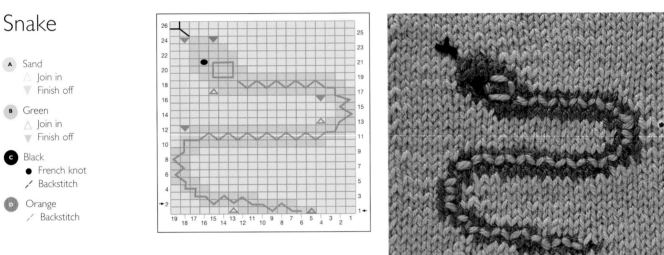

Use on: Hat, baby sweater

Frog

A Pale aqua
△ Join in
▽ Finish off
Backstitch

B Dark green
△ Join in
▽ Finish off

C Light green
△ Join in
▽ Finish off

D Black
● French knot

E Orange
○ Single chain stitch

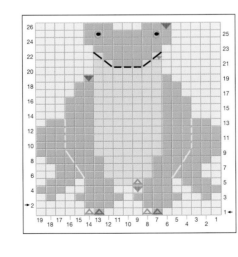

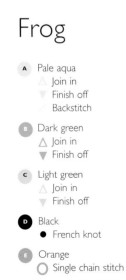

Use on: Hat, baby sweater

Large fish

A Turquoise
  △ Join in
  ▽ Finish off

B Orange
  △ Join in
  ▽ Finish off

C Pale turquoise
  Join in
  Finish off

D Dark green
  ╱ Backstitch
  ∨ Duplicate stitch
  ● French knot

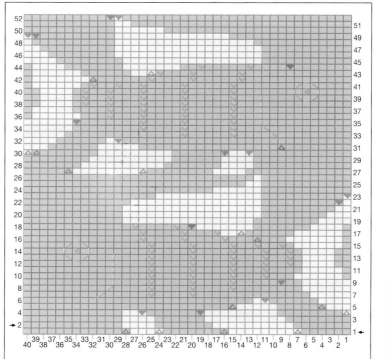

SEE ALSO
Backstitch, page 50
Single chain stitch, page 51
Duplicate stitch, page 52
French knots, page 52

Use on: Tote bag,
one-panel cushion

Small ted

A Pale aqua
△ Join in
▽ Finish off

B Golden brown
△ Join in
▽ Finish off

C Royal blue
△ Join in
▽ Finish off

D Black
╱ Backstitch
● French knot

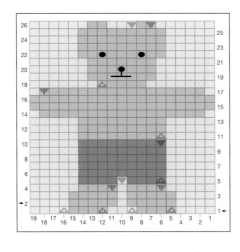

Use on: Baby blanket, four-panel cushion, baby sweater

Balloons

A Pale aqua
△ Join in
▽ Finish off

B Red
△ Join in
▽ Finish off
╱ Backstitch

C Blue
△ Join in
▽ Finish off
╱ Backstitch
✕ Sew on bow made with 8 inches (20cm) braid, or ribbon (blue on red balloon, red on blue)

D White
△ Join in
▽ Finish off

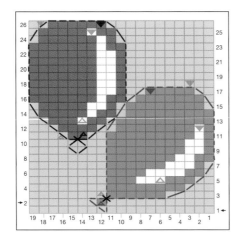

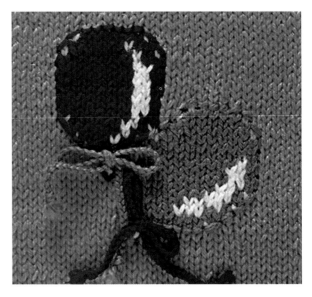

Use on: Scarf, hat, baby blanket, four-panel cushion

Kite

A Pale blue
△ Join in
▽ Finish off

B Royal blue
△ Join in
▽ Finish off

C Red
△ Join in
▽ Finish off
✕ Sew on bow made with 8 inches (20cm) braid in red, or ribbon

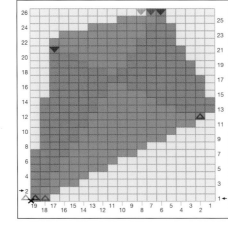

Use on: Four-panel cushion, baby blanket, baby sweater

Large ted

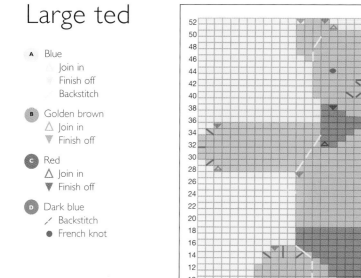

A Blue
△ Join in
▽ Finish off
Backstitch

B Golden brown
△ Join in
▽ Finish off

C Red
△ Join in
▽ Finish off

D Dark blue
╱ Backstitch
● French knot

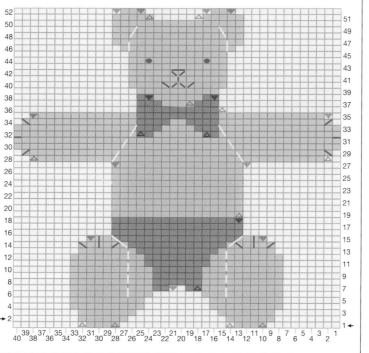

SEE ALSO
Braids, page 32
Backstitch, page 50
French knots, page 52

Use on: Tote bag, child's sweater

Boat

A Denim blue
△ Join in
▽ Finish off
∨ Duplicate stitch

B Red
△ Join in
▽ Finish off

C White
△ Join in
▽ Finish off

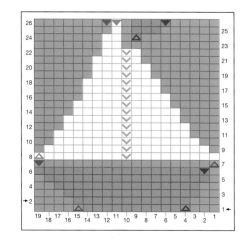

Use on: Hat, baby blanket, four-panel cushion, baby sweater

Plane

A Turquoise
△ Join in
▽ Finish off

B Pale gray-blue
△ Join in
▽ Finish off

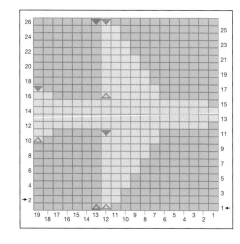

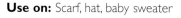

Use on: Scarf, hat, baby sweater

Helicopter

A Denim blue
△ Join in
▽ Finish off

B Black
△ Join in
▼ Finish off
∨ Duplicate stitch

C Red
△ Join in
▽ Finish off
∨ Duplicate stitch

D Pale gray-blue
△ Join in
▽ Finish off

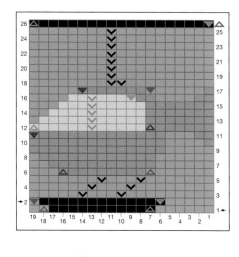

Use on: Baby sweater

Pirate ship

A Turquoise
△ Join in
▽ Finish off

B Golden brown
△ Join in
▽ Finish off
╱ Backstitch

C Red
△ Join in
▽ Finish off

D White
△ Join in
▽ Finish off

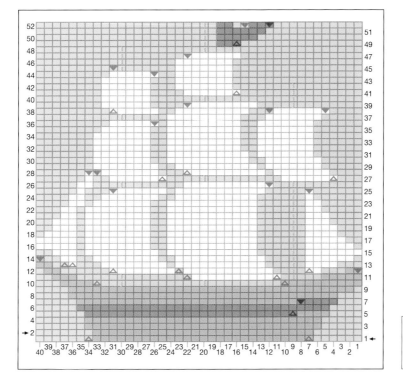

SEE ALSO
Backstitch, page 50
Duplicate stitch, page 52

Use on: One-panel
cushion, child's sweater

Adding lettering

Add any name or slogan to your knitting, following these simple steps:

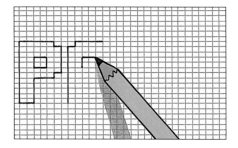

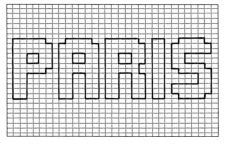

Step 1

Photocopy the large grid from page 123. Use a pencil to copy the letters you want onto the grid. Leave one blank rectangle between the letters. (Leave three or four blank rectangles between words, or put the words on different lines.) You can color in your chart to make it easier to read.

Step 2

Count the stitches required for the width of your lettering. The letters are 12 rows high. Decide where to place the lettering on your knitting, so the lettering will start on a right side row (see page 79).

TIP

On a sweater, any lettering (or other motif) looks good if you center it level with the beginning of the armhole shaping.

Step 3

Use one ball of background color and float it across the wrong side (see page 41). You can float the contrast color in the same way across the back of five (or six) stitches or less. Where the gap is more than six stitches it is better to join in a separate ball, to avoid puckering.

Step 4

If you want to work each letter in a different color, you can still use just one ball of background color and float it across the wrong side.

Alphabet

 White

B Red

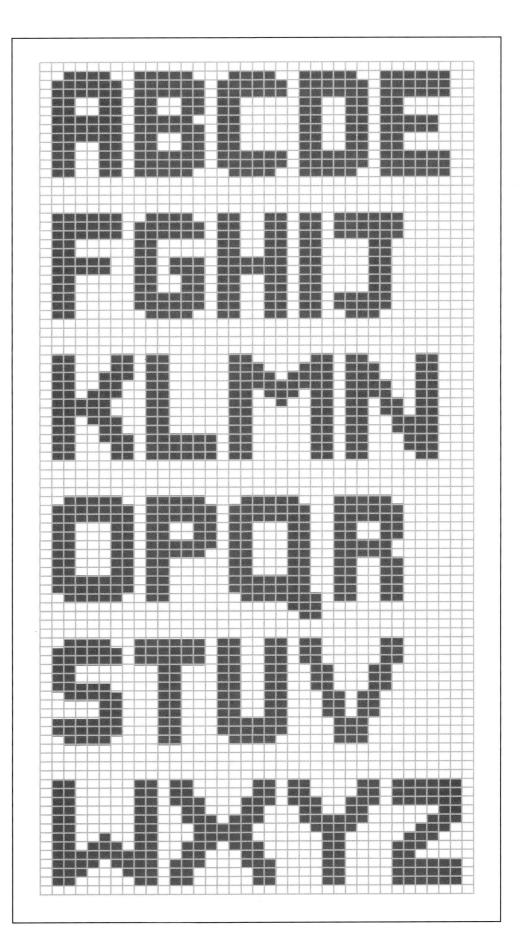

Draw your own motif

Use our blank grid to design your own motifs. This grid is the same size as the one used for the motifs in this book, so you can design your own picture for any of our projects.

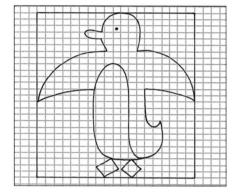

Step 1

Photocopy the grid from the opposite page. Use a pencil to lightly sketch the outline of your design.

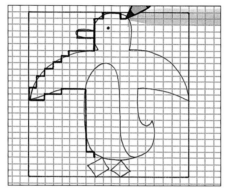

Step 2

Redraw the outlines, following the rectangles on the grid. Sloping lines and curves will be stepped. On a straight sloping line, arrange the steps as evenly as you can. When you are happy with the stepped lines, draw over them in black pen and erase all the pencil marks.

Step 3

Lightly color in your design: use colored pencils, so the grid lines remain visible. If your picture includes small details or fine lines, decide whether to knit these in, duplicate stitch them later, or embroider them with other stitches.

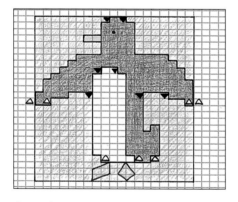

Step 4

As you knit, you can mark on your chart the symbols for joining in   and for finishing off   in case you want to use the chart again in the future.

TIP

For a large design, you can tape several photocopied grids together. Number the rows to help you follow the chart accurately.

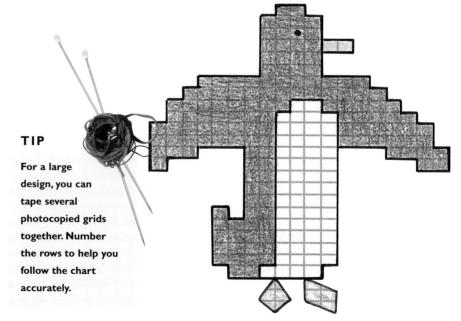

Glossary

3-ply, 4-ply light-weight knitting yarns, sometimes called fingering.

acrylic a synthetic fiber.

Angora very soft yarn fiber made from the combed fur of the Angora rabbit, usually blended with other fibers.

Aran-weight a medium- to heavy-weight yarn. Also known as fisherman's yarn.

backstitch a firm sewing stitch, also used to embroider fine lines and outlines.

bamboo fiber from the bamboo plant, used to make a smooth, silky yarn; also the woody stem, used to make knitting needles.

binding off fastening off stitches so they will not unravel.

block, blocking treating a piece of knitting (by washing and/or pressing) to set its shape.

bobbin a plastic or cardboard holder for a small amount of yarn.

bouclé yarn a fancy yarn with a knobbly effect.

bulky a heavy-weight yarn, sometimes called chunky.

button band or button border a separate band, knitted sideways or lengthwise, to which buttons are sewn.

buttonhole band or buttonhole border a separate band, knitted sideways or lengthwise, with buttonholes worked as knitting proceeds.

casting on making new stitches on a needle.

chain stitch an embroidery stitch, used for medium-width, curved lines.

chenille a type of yarn that makes a velvety texture when knitted.

chunky a heavy-weight yarn, sometimes called bulky.

cotton a natural fiber derived from the cotton plant.

cuff the lower border of a sleeve.

decreasing working stitches together to reduce their number.

double knitting a medium-weight yarn.

double-pointed needle a knitting needle with a point at each end.

duplicate stitch an embroidery stitch that copies knitted stitches, also known as Swiss darning.

dyelot number indicates the exact dye bath used, not just the shade.

fingering a fine-weight yarn (similar to 3-ply and 4-ply).

float the strand of yarn left at the wrong side of the work when stranding across several stitches.

French knot an embroidery stitch forming a small rounded knot, used for eyes and other dot details.

fully-fashioned shaping shaping emphasized by working decreases (or increases) two or more stitches in from the edge of the work.

garter stitch formed by working all stitches as knit on every row.

gauge the number of stitches and rows to a given measurement.

hank a coil of yarn.

increasing making extra stitches.

intarsia another name for picture knitting.

invisible seam method of joining knitted pieces with mattress stitch.

knitwise as when knitting a stitch.

knop a textured yarn with occasional large bumps.

linen a natural fiber derived from the flax plant.

lurex a metallic fiber used to make yarn, either alone or blended with other fibers.

mattress stitch the stitch used for the invisible seam.

mohair a natural fiber, hair from the Angora goat.

natural fiber fiber naturally occurring as an animal or vegetable product.

needle gauge a small metal or plastic sheet with holes of different sizes, labeled with needle sizes, for checking the size of knitting needles.

pattern a stitch pattern, or a set of instructions for making a garment.

pearl cotton a slightly glossy embroidery thread suitable for use on knitting.

polyamide (nylon) a synthetic fiber.

polyester a synthetic fiber.

purlwise as when purling a stitch.

ramie fiber from the ramie plant, used to make a smooth, cool yarn.

reverse stockinette stitch stockinette stitch worked with the purl side as the right side.

rib stitches or ribbing various combinations of knit and purl stitches, arranged to form vertical lines.

right and left (when describing parts of a garment) describes where the garment part will be when worn, for example, the right sleeve is the sleeve worn on the right arm, not the sleeve on the right when you look at the garment from the front.

right side the side of the work that will be outside the garment when worn.

ring marker a smooth, unbroken ring of metal or plastic, slipped onto a needle to mark a particular position along a row, and slipped from row to row as knitting proceeds.

seam the join made when two pieces of knitting are sewn together.

seed stitch a stitch pattern with a "dotted" appearance.

selvage stitch the first or last stitch of a row worked in a different way to the rest of the row, to make a decorative edge, or a firm, neat edge for seaming.

sequins flat shapes cut from metallic foil, sewn on as decoration.

set-in sleeve a sleeve and armhole shaping where the armhole is curved to take a curved sleeve head.

shaping increasing or decreasing the number of stitches to form the shape required.

Shetland wool loosely spun wool from sheep from the Shetland Islands.

silk a natural fiber from the cocoon of the silkworm.

single chain stitch an embroidery stitch often used for flower petals.

slip stitch a stitch slipped from one needle to the other without working into it, or a simple sewing stitch taking one strand from one edge and one strand from the other.

slub yarn or slubby yarn yarn of uneven thickness.

soft cotton a heavy-weight embroidery thread suitable for use on knitting.

sport-weight a medium-weight yarn similar to double knitting.

stitch holder a device used for holding stitches temporarily.

stitch marker a split ring of metal or plastic, slipped onto a knitted stitch to mark a position.

stockinette stitch formed by working one row of knit stitches, one row of purl stitches, and repeating these two rows.

straight stitch a single embroidered stitch, used for details such as whiskers.

stranding carrying a color to a new position across the wrong side of the work.

Swiss darning another term for duplicate stitch.

synthetic fiber manufactured fiber, not naturally occurring.

tapestry needle a sewing needle with a blunt tip and a large eye.

tapestry wool wool sold for embroidery, similar in weight to double knitting.

tweed yarn yarn spun with flecks of contrasting colors, to resemble tweed fabric.

viscose rayon a man-made fiber derived from cellulose.

wool a natural fiber from the coat of sheep.

wrong side the side of the work that will be inside the garment when worn.

Index